PRAISE FOR THE BOOK

"An invaluable resource for all educators, *On the Edge of Their Seats* focuses on the heart of successful teaching: reaching our students. It is accessible, practical, and inspirational. This book provides tools and ideas I can implement in my classroom now and in the years to come." **Caris Zeller, Chemistry Teacher, Glenbard East High School**

"*On the Edge of Their Seats* presents a clearly articulated and jargon-free alternative to the standard 'best practices' approach to teaching. All too often, we lose sight of the intrinsic value of what is being taught and its connection to the commitments and passions of both teachers and students. Given the demoralized climate of today's teaching profession, there is a pressing need to reaffirm the transformative potential of teaching for those who care deeply about what and whom they teach. This is what Jonas and Yacek do here, and in a clear, accessible, and engaging manner." **Dini Metro-Roland, Professor of Education, Western Michigan University**

"Jonas and Yacek proffer a unique approach to the art of teaching that is undergirded by solid educational research. Their four-step approach is effectively presented, and then uniquely supported with exemplary classroom scenarios. In sum, they provide educators a dynamic paradigm for examining how to promote better student engagement and the value of learning for learning's sake!" **Thomas Greene, Former Assistant Superintendent Beaverton Public Schools, and Former Provost University of Portland**

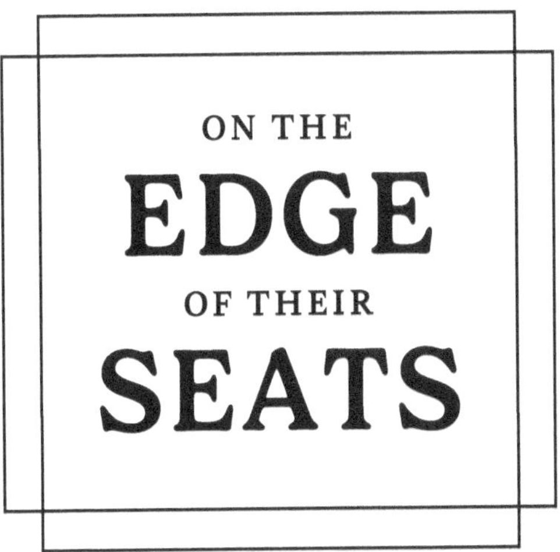

# ON THE EDGE OF THEIR SEATS

## What the Best Teachers Do to Engage and Inspire Their Students

MARK E. JONAS
&
DOUGLAS W. YACEK

POST & LINTEL BOOKS
CHICAGO

Published in the United States by Post & Lintel Books, Chicago.
10 9 8 7 6 5 4 3 2 1



Library of Congress Cataloging-in-Publication Data
Names: Jonas, Mark E.  author.
Title: On the edge of their seats: What the best teachers do to engage and inspire their students / Mark E. Jonas and Douglas W. Yacek
Description: Chicago: Post & Lintel Books, 2023
p.  cm.
Includes bibliographical references
Identifiers: LCCN 2023923399
ISBN 979-8-9894440-0-7 (paperback) | ISBN 979-8-9894440-2-1 (hardcover)
ISBN 979-8-9894440-3-8 (epub)
LC record available at https://lccn.loc.gov/2023923399

www.postandlintelbooks.com

Book cover design by Evelyn Li
Typeset in Valkyrie, Font Copyright © Mattew Butterick.

FOR OUR STUDENTS

# Contents

# Introduction

## *Our Educational Predicament*

IT WAS THE FINAL day of a team-building retreat put on by the English department, and the school year was just around the corner. The discussion up to that point had revolved around the usual topics: course assignments, curricular changes, and student discipline. We were all feeling exhausted by the discussion and were more than ready to head home. But just as the day was ending, the conversation took an unexpected turn.

A colleague began telling the story of an unforgettable experience he had just as he was finishing his student teaching. His supervisor suggested he shadow a student for a day, instead of a fellow teacher. The idea sounded interesting, and he decided to embark on his shadow experience later that week.

What awaited him was chilling. Class after class followed the same tired formula: show up, take roll, listen to the teacher, complete an individual or small group activity, write down the homework assignment. Then the bell rang; everyone shuffled to a new location—and five minutes later the formula repeated. He realized that hundreds of students at his school went through that same mind-numbing routine day in and day out. He promised himself that he would make his classes different. And yet he wasn't certain he was offering anything beyond the formula. He followed the newest trends in classroom pedagogy—fishbowl discussions, think-pair-shares, literature circles—and frequently implemented them. But in spite of his efforts, he confessed that he sometimes felt bored by his own classes, and his students seemed bored as well.

We have spoken with hundreds of students, teachers, and parents who tell the same story.[1] Although educators over the last several decades have made important strides in developing effective methods of instruction, many students still experience their education as a series of dull and uninspiring classes that they simply must endure.[2] Students may learn the material, but they do not want to learn it. They go through the motions, but they rarely see the value of their education beyond checking boxes for graduation or improving their career prospects.

It should be no surprise that student disengagement has become a prevailing feature of education in the 21st century, with disengagement levels rising dramatically as students reach higher grades and progress through college.[3] Disengagement is not confined to any particular demographic group. It affects students in urban, suburban, and rural schools; in wealthy and poor schools; in public and charter schools; and in majority white schools as well as those composed largely of students of color.[4] This trend is troubling not only because disengaged students learn less and set lower expectations for themselves. They also have less hope for their future and are more likely to drop out of school.[5]

Although disengagement touches the lives of every demographic group in US schools, it does not impact them equally. Urban students, poor students, students of color, and other marginalized groups face distinctive challenges during their time in school. They are more likely to be suspended from school, misdiagnosed with learning disabilities, and exposed to social stigmas and stereotypes. When these challenges are compounded by disengaging and uninspired instruction, their effects become particularly acute.[6] Every day that teachers fail to engage their at-risk students deals another blow to the goals of diversity, equity, and inclusion—goals for which our educational system ought to stand.

What can we do about our educational predicament? Can teachers transform the educational experience of their students? Can they make their classrooms places of inspiration and engagement? Can they reach the students who have the greatest need?

We believe they can. Nearly all the students, teachers, and parents we've spoken to over the years describe exceptions to the drudgery—teachers who brought life to the classroom, communicated a passion for their subjects, and made students excited to come to class. This book is about what makes these teachers exceptional and how other teachers might follow their lead. It is about what teachers need to do to bring students consistently to *the edge of their seats*.

## *What We Mean by the "Best"*

In our view, the best teachers are not necessarily the ones who perfectly execute their lesson plans, effortlessly manage their classrooms, or expertly avoid instructional mistakes. When we talk about the "best teachers," we are not thinking as much about *performance* as we are about *character*. What separates the best from the rest is a professional commitment: The best teachers are dedicated to continually improving their teaching. They want students to cherish their time in class and to love what they are learning. They want students to reach their highest potential, and sometimes to realize that they have this potential in the first place. Finally, they want their students to grow as moral beings, as citizens, and as shapers of their own future.

There is tremendous diversity among the teachers who accomplish these goals with students. No book and no framework for teaching could ever do complete justice to this diversity. And yet there are several instructional elements that appear again and again in the most effective classrooms. This book lays out these elements so that teachers can put them to use in their own classes.

## *Our Approach*

In our almost three decades of experience in teacher education and professional development, we have found that the best teachers consistently use four instructional strategies or steps. We call these steps the *Hook*, the *Pitch*, the *Awakening*, and the *Strengthening*. As we will show in the following chapters, these four steps are effective for increasing student engagement at the middle school, high school, and college level.

Teachers who use the four steps consistently describe their students as being highly motivated in their classes. Their students express excitement about coming to class; they participate with enthusiasm and focus; and they leave class talking to their friends and parents about what they have learned. They begin to see scientific theories, poetic devices, mathematical concepts, historical events, and sociological theories not only as "instructive" and "important for the next exam," but as objects of fascination and even wonder. There is palpable energy in these classes, and students show up expecting important learning to occur. In our terms, these teachers bring students to the edge of their seats.

The four-step approach is *not* about amusing or entertaining students, however. Its central purpose is genuine engagement and inspiration. Of course, students might describe lessons or courses that bring them to the edge of their seats as "exciting" or "fun," but they will be much more. The best teachers help students recognize the unique and enduring value of subject matter for their lives. They help students see the world and themselves in a richer and more personally fulfilling way. The four steps help teachers produce this kind of experience on a consistent basis.

In the following chapters, we present the characteristic features of the four steps along with numerous examples of teachers who have successfully implemented them in their classroom. These examples are inspired by the hundreds of teachers we have interviewed, observed, and mentored over the years. We have created these examples to represent a variety of academic disciplines, grade levels, school types, class sizes, and demographic makeups. This diversity is intentional. The four-step framework is suitable for application in a variety of academic settings beginning in middle school and extending through college. This wide applicability is what makes our approach truly unique. Whether in middle-class or working-class schools, in predominantly black, brown, or white communities, we have found that the best teachers consistently use the four steps to engage and inspire their students. Of course, the specific methods and materials that teachers use vary depending on their cultural context, but the basic elements of instruction remain the same.

The step-by-step guidance offered in this book should not be understood as an exact recipe for classroom instruction—the kind often found in guidebooks for teachers. Given the wide range of educational settings and student backgrounds in US schools, it is impossible to provide such a recipe. Instead, we show how teachers can develop their own distinct approaches to engaging their students with the help of the four-step framework. We think this method of presentation is more respectful of teachers' professional expertise than the recipe approach, and it also emphasizes the importance of teachers' personal styles in creating deeply engaging and inspiring lessons.

## *Research-Based Teaching*

The four-step framework is based on several important research developments in education over the last decade.

Foremost among these is the research on student engagement. What factors most impact student engagement?—the research on this question is remarkably clear. The single most significant factor influencing student engagement is the teacher.[7] School-wide policies and procedures can certainly support (or undermine) student engagement, and conditions in students' home lives play an important role as well. But it is teachers themselves—the quality of instruction they provide and the classroom conditions they create—that set the tone and trajectory of the learning environment and largely determine its potential.

In addition to these findings, the recent research on transformative teaching and learning has generated several key insights into effective and engaging instruction.[8] This research has shown that teachers in contemporary schools can initiate powerful shifts of perspective and feeling in their students called *transformative experiences*.[9] These experiences occur when students begin to see how school subjects can expand and enrich their everyday experience and contribute to a growing capacity for understanding and wonder.[10] Researchers have shown that transformative experiences—far from being one-off moments of insight—can be consistently integrated into the day-to-day business of teaching and learning.[11]

One of the most important results of this research is the connection researchers have established between transformative experiences and student learning. Students who have had transformative experiences with subject matter are more likely to perform well on assessments, engage in learning activities, and understand course concepts in a deep way.[12]

Moreover, transformative experiences indicate that a special *kind* of learning has taken place. Students moved by such experiences grasp the profound personal significance that subject matter can have for their lives, and they want to explore its potential further. In this way, transformative experiences bridge the school-life divide that so often characterizes students' experience in the classroom.

Transformative experiences with subject matter play a central role in the four-step framework. In essence, our approach spells out how teachers can model the ways they have been inspired, fascinated, and transformed by their own subjects so that they can prepare students to be similarly transformed.[13]

## *Who This Book Is For*

We have written this book for teachers who want their students to be truly excited about their classes. Our readers might be teachers who love teaching and want to love it more, who used to love teaching and want to rediscover that love, or who are burned out and want to rescue their career.

As any teacher knows, teaching fully engaged students is one of the most rewarding experiences a teacher can have. When students are actively participating and contributing to the class, the result is almost magical. Students discuss the course material with subtlety and depth; they encourage one another's questions and observations; they share personal experiences and develop lasting relationships with each other and their teachers. Engaged students not only learn better and register higher levels of satisfaction with school. They are also more likely to live up to their potential as learners and as people.

When students are deflated and disengaged, however, teaching becomes a chore. Lessons seem interminable, and the classroom feels devoid of life. If these conditions last long enough, teachers exhibit increasing levels of indifference, occupational stress, and burnout.

We hope this book will provide teachers with inspiration and guidance for increasing student engagement in their classes—for the sake of teachers and their students.

# 2

# Getting Started with the Framework

WHAT DO TEACHERS need to do to begin increasing student engagement in their classrooms? How can they bring students to the edge of their seats? In this chapter, we provide an overview of the four instructional steps that effective teachers use to make their classrooms places of engagement, inspiration, and transformation. We also discuss several important prerequisites for teachers who want to begin applying the framework in their lessons and classes today.

## *The Four-Step Framework*

The four-step framework draws on several powerful methods proven to engage students' attention and interest in the classroom.

The first step of the framework is called the *Hook*. The *Hook* is a series of actions a teacher performs to capture students' attention and interest in the first moments of a course or lesson. They might arrange their classroom space in an unusual way, use out-of-the-box ways of framing the goals and tasks of the class, recite provocative quotes, or draw on powerful and engaging examples of course ideas. The purpose of the *Hook* is *not* to make the first moments or days of class entertaining, as already mentioned. An effective *Hook* surprises students; it challenges their expectations about how class will be conducted and provokes how they see the world. The *Hook* communicates that the course will be more than just another math, English, or science class. It suggests something unique is going to take place here.

The second step is called the *Pitch*. The *Pitch* is a series of actions a teacher performs to direct students' attention towards the "intrinsic value" of subject matter—that is, how it might be seen as compelling, interesting, and fascinating on its own terms. Whereas the *Hook* primarily focuses students' attention on the *teacher's* behaviors, the *Pitch* shifts emphasis to the *course content* itself. Teachers might highlight the subject matter's beauty or profundity, tell personal stories of its role in their own lives, or demonstrate its significance in natural or human history. The *Pitch* is not a presentation of the subject matter's relevance for finding a job, getting into a good college, or preparing for next year's classes, however. Rather, it highlights the subject's innate capacity to intrigue and inspire. In effective *Pitches,* teachers not only exhibit their own passion and interest in subject matter; they also assure students that they too can develop a deep passion and interest in the subject. This sets the stage for the powerful shift of perspective that occurs in the next step.

The third step is called the *Awakening*. The *Awakening*

is a series of actions a teacher performs to create profound moments of insight into the transformative power of subject matter. Whereas the *Pitch* draws students' attention to the *potential* of the subject matter to be inspiring, the *Awakening* turns that potential into a reality. Students who experience an *Awakening* see firsthand what the subject really has to offer. They experience its meaning, its significance, its power, not in the abstract but for their lives. Teachers might use a carefully crafted class discussion, an evocative film scene, or a compelling first-person narrative to facilitate this experience. The purpose of the *Awakening* is not merely to create an "Aha" moment, however. The goal is to construct what we might call an "Oh, wow" experience, in which students recognize for themselves how the subject matter can enrich their lives. When students experience an *Awakening*, it often marks turning points in their relationship to the course material. They rethink their assumptions about the world, the subject, or other people, and they begin to reconsider who they are as individuals. Because such transformative shifts of perspective create an especially deep and enduring form of engagement, the *Awakening* forms the heart of our framework.

The fourth step is called the *Strengthening*. The *Strengthening* is a series of actions a teacher performs to deepen and expand the insights gained in the *Awakening*. Whereas the *Awakening* yields a new appreciation of the subject matter, the *Strengthening* helps it become a stable motivator of student learning. The teacher might assign a student-directed project, organize a field trip, or plan a debate that students prepare for over several days and weeks. The purpose of the *Strengthening* is not only to help students connect more robustly to the course content, but to experience the transformative power of the *Awakenings* in their own lives. In effective *Strengthenings*, teachers give ample space for students to apply the insights they've gained throughout the course and pursue related interests, topics, and experiences. Ultimately, successful *Strengthenings* create a classroom community in which students feel united in pursuing the subject discipline for further growth as people.

The table on the following page (Table 1) outlines these steps as well as the actions teachers can take to implement them in the classroom. The full explanation of these steps will be provided as we move through the chapters of this book.

Although this framework organizes the phases of effective instruction into discrete steps, they often overlap with each other in practice. Successful *Hooks* will almost always foreshadow aspects of the *Pitch*, as well as set the stage for the *Awakening* and *Strengthening*. Similarly, the *Pitch* or *Awakening* will often take up elements of the *Hook*. Nevertheless, it will be helpful for teachers to plan these steps separately in the initial stages of applying the framework.

## *Prerequisite #1: What Students Really Want*

The four steps provide a comprehensive approach to designing highly engaging courses and lessons. Of course, this doesn't

| | GOAL | METHODS |
|---|---|---|
| **THE HOOK** | … engages student attention and promotes curiosity toward subject matter as well as the teacher's approach to teaching | … uses out-of-the-box introductory activities and attention-grabbing teacher behaviors, dress, classroom structure, or novel approaches to curriculum design |
| **THE PITCH** | … focuses student attention on subject matter as a potential source of intrinsic value and personal significance | … uses personal stories or anecdotes about subject matter, expressions of passion and fascination for the subject, or affirmations of student learning potential |
| **THE AWAKENING** | … enables students to encounter a significant insight into the nature of the subject matter and its potential role in their lives | … uses leading questions that close in on a result or finding, expressions of excitement toward the direct goal in view, or encouragements of students' contributions to the result of the lesson |
| **THE STRENGTHENING** | … strengthens students' newly gained insight and promotes a lasting commitment to personal enrichment | … uses activities that help students reflect on their *Awakenings*, discuss their insights with others, and pursue their best selves beyond the curriculum or course material |

Table 1. The Four-Step Framework

mean that the four steps cover *everything* the most engaging teachers do. We have found that the four-step framework is most successful when teachers attend to several "prerequisites" for student engagement in their classrooms. The first involves how teachers think about their students. Bringing students to the edge of their seats starts with the belief that students want—deep down—to be inspired by what they are learning. Of course, students may sometimes actively resist their teachers' efforts, fixing their minds on anything else but their academics. Students are often preoccupied with their social lives, unprepared for class, distracted by technology, or lacking basic study skills. Yet these outward behaviors do not reflect students' deepest desires. Young people *want* to have meaningful experiences in the classroom. They *want* to be moved by the subjects they are studying. They *want* to be shown how these subjects can enrich their experience and help them appreciate the splendor of the world around them.

Many contemporary schools work against teachers' efforts to speak to these deeper desires for learning. Schools often operate on the logic of future preparation, which says that education should provide young people with the knowledge and skills they will need for educational advancement, a lucrative career, and material prosperity. We do not deny that preparing students for a successful future is important. In fact, the four steps aim for deep engagement rather than mere entertainment in part because this is what prepares students best for their future. Genuine engagement not only leads to better academic performance and greater social mobility; it also encourages virtues such as attentiveness, diligence, perseverance, and curiosity that students will need later in life. If we want to prepare students for their future, the best way to do so is to help them fully engage in their classes.

However, engaging young people just for the sake of their future is to deny them an equally important aspect of education. Education should also be about enriching their *current* lives. It should help them see the beauty and richness of the world around them. It should help them recognize the value and dignity of every human being. And it should help them become people of character and purpose. These further educational aims connect to common human desires for meaning and fulfillment in life, and we do our students a disservice if we ignore them. After all, we compel young people to be in school during the best hours of their day, during the most formative years of their lives—taking these desires seriously is the least we can do.

## *Prerequisite #2:*
## *The Hardest Class They've Ever Taken*

The second feature of highly engaging classrooms involves the culture teachers intentionally create there. Bringing students to the edge of their seats requires hard work not only from teachers, but also from students. It urges students to open their hearts and minds to completely new ways of thinking about academic subjects and to engage more deeply with the material than they ever have before. In fact, students often refer to classes designed with this framework as some of the hardest they've ever taken.

We have found that the most successful teachers build a

classroom culture that embraces academic struggle. Students will have to learn to enjoy, even relish, the challenge of education.[14] At first glance, this might seem to be a disadvantage of the framework. Can we really bring young people *this* far toward appreciating what they learn in school? We think so. In fact, we have found that raising the academic bar in the classroom has a tremendous motivational effect on students. Students value their learning much more when they feel like they have earned it. Their learning becomes their own.[15] When teachers intentionally create a culture that celebrates challenge, students start to see themselves as having greater agency and autonomy in their own learning.[16] They feel empowered.[17]

Teachers shouldn't be surprised if students initially resist their efforts to raise expectations in their classrooms. They shouldn't give up if their students complain about how challenging the class is or how much effort they're putting in. In a certain sense, these complaints can be a sign of success. They show that students are having to adjust to the high expectations of their teachers and grapple with the material much more deeply than they do in less demanding classes.

This is not to say that students should be left alone with their academic struggles. High standards facilitate student engagement when students feel supported and cared for by their teachers and when they have been equipped with the resources to achieve these standards.

Ultimately, the goal is to create a classroom culture that is appropriately challenging and supportive. Concrete ideas for how to create this kind of classroom culture are integrated throughout this book.

## *Prerequisite #3: The Power of Persona*

A third prerequisite for teachers has to do with their personal style of instruction. The importance of finding one's personal style in teaching cannot be overstated. We have found that teachers who carefully choose how they act in the classroom, how they speak to students, and even what they wear will be far more likely to engage their students at the highest level. In this book, we refer to these intentional choices about the teacher's classroom presence as the teacher's *persona*.

The teacher's persona is different from their normal personality. We often think of our personalities as fixed dimensions of our character. In reality our personalities shift a great deal between different contexts. At work we often act differently than with our friends; with family we act differently than with strangers, and so on. It is the same in the classroom. When we teach, we think and behave in ways unique to the teaching environment.

This is where the concept of persona comes in. Typically, we think of a persona as something actors adopt when they are playing a role on stage. The persona here is divorced from each actor's actual personality. This is not how we use the word "persona." For us, a persona is a version of ourselves made up of one or more aspects of our personality that we intentionally choose to highlight or diminish in our classrooms. To use an analogy: instead of saying, "I'm just going to be me in the classroom," the teacher adopting a persona asks, "Which *version* of me will most effectively engage my students in the deepest way?" Sometimes the "me" a teacher chooses will be similar to who they are in other contexts; but other times it will be radically different. In the latter case, they are not making up a different personality, but simply choosing to put forward a variation of themselves that will best resonate with the students and help them connect to the curriculum.

The examples in later chapters will help readers understand how teachers can develop and employ personas within the four-step process. In many cases, we show how the teachers developed their personas over time. Presenting this development not only emphasizes the ways personas contribute to a compelling classroom experience; it also demonstrates that any teacher can create an engaging persona from their own personality.

## *Prerequisite #4:*
## *Taking the Long View*

The final prerequisite for applying the framework has to do with teachers' expectations of success and failure in using the four steps. Increasing student engagement is rarely something we can achieve overnight. It is often a career-long endeavor, requiring patience, diligence, commitment, and—when things don't go quite as planned—hope. The steps we provide in this book can dramatically increase engagement in students, but progress will be incremental. While a few teachers might be able to immediately implement the four steps with marked success, most teachers will need to work at them over weeks, months, and even years. Teachers should not be worried if their attempts are not as successful as the examples we have created in this book. These teachers are often depicted as having spent years working on these steps and experienced many setbacks along the way. It was the same for many of the outstandings teachers we have met in the past and will be so for the majority of teachers who use this framework in the future.

That said, there is a way to shorten the time it takes to become proficient in each of the four steps: *rehearse, rehearse, rehearse*. Rehearsal is a forgotten art in teaching. The single most important thing a teacher can do to create effective *Hooks, Pitches, Awakenings,* and *Strengthenings* is to practice them before the students show up in class. Rehearsing these four steps does not guarantee they will be effective, of course. But it significantly improves the odds.

Some will prefer practicing in front of a mirror; some will do it in an empty classroom; some will want to rehearse in front of friends or family. However it's done, we believe that part of the rehearsing should involve imagining how students will respond. Will this setup grab their attention? Is this joke going to land? Will my approach be distinct enough to students? How would I feel if I did this activity? Do I sound as convinced about the importance of the subject as I feel?

When teachers rehearse the four steps, something crucial for the success of their lessons occurs. They no longer need to fixate on what they actually say or do in class, or on what they need to say or do next. This frees up their minds to notice students' body language and verbal responses so that they can adjust their teaching accordingly.

When teachers rehearse, they also gain confidence. If teachers rehearse their first-day *Hook,* for example, several times before they actually see their students, it can feel like they have done it before, which makes them less nervous.

However, it is important *not to memorize* how we want the class to go. The goal of rehearsals is to get a *feel* for the various moves in the four steps, not to lock them down. In fact, when teachers too rigidly stick to practiced lines and transitions, this can make their teaching seem wooden or mechanical, preventing them from adapting to students' immediate responses and needs. Mechanical teaching almost never leads to student engagement; it often leads away from it.

The most important way teachers can prevent their rehearsals from becoming mechanical is to never write down exactly what they will say. Using a script leads to the memorization of words, which quickly becomes rigid and formulaic. The goal is to rehearse the *basic ideas* over and over again, even if the *exact words* used are slightly different every time. Doing this makes the ideas permanent, but allows their expression to remain spontaneous. When the class begins, teachers know roughly what they want to say, but *how* they say it will always be fresh.

Rehearsing may feel awkward at first for those of us who have never done it, but once teachers get the hang of it, they will wonder why they hadn't started it earlier.

## *Applying the Framework*

Some readers may wonder whether this framework is realistic. Do we really believe that students can be excited about what we teach? Can they come to value the subject matter in the profound and transformative way we are suggesting?

Can they be brought consistently to the edge of their seats? Can teachers achieve these goals while also addressing the numerous institutional requirements placed upon them?

They can. We are not saying it will be easy, or that teachers will succeed with every student. The four steps take hard work, creativity, collaboration, insight, and a little bit of luck. There will be false starts, mistakes, and setbacks along the way. But when teachers persevere, something almost magical can happen in their classrooms. Students come alive and begin loving what they learn. They begin to see themselves as capable and competent people who can take on difficult challenges and achieve their aspirations. And they become curious about the world and about how they can make it a better place.

To watch students develop in this way is rewarding beyond comparison. It can fill a teacher with a deeper sense of meaning and a renewed hope for the world. This is why we think bringing students to the edge of their seats is teaching and learning at its best.

# The Hook

THE START OF A SCHOOL year is full of excitement and energy. Students cheerfully catch up with old friends; nervously examine campus maps to find their classes; or eagerly scan the classroom for friends or acquaintances. When students do each of these things, they are already "engaged" in school. The problem is that this degree of engagement doesn't usually extend to the academic side of their school experience.

In fact, students often have quite negative expectations about what will happen in the classroom and how much will be demanded of them. Many assume that class will be business as usual, requiring little in the way of genuine engagement and effort. Unfortunately, their expectations often come true.

When teachers use a *Hook,* they disrupt these expectations. They intentionally use the first moments of a class or lesson to show students that *this* class will be different. A *Hook* suggests that something deeply significant will occur during this class, something beyond the day-to-day grind of school or college. It hints at the new insights students will gain.

The best way to understand the *Hook* is to see it in action. Let's take a look at two teachers who employ several essential features of the *Hook*: James, a high school English teacher, and Mariela, a middle school science teacher. Both teachers were able to create effective instructional *Hooks* despite several initial challenges and setbacks.

## *The Hook in Action: James' High School English Class*

When James decided later in life to become a high school English teacher, he didn't have a vision for what his teaching would look like. He was excited about leaving his unfulfilling job as a consultant and getting to work with young people. But when he started his M.A.T. program, he was underwhelmed by what he encountered. He was introduced to a set of methods for leading discussions, managing the classroom, and designing effective assessments. He could see that these methods might make his own classes more engaging than the ones he experienced as a student, but he felt that something important was still missing. The methods seemed lifeless to him.

Toward the end of his studies, one of James' professors advised him to re-watch the movie *Dead Poets Society*. James was initially put off by the suggestion. He had heard strong criticisms of the movie for its unrealistic portrayal of the classroom, so he had fairly low expectations when he sat down to watch the film. Sure enough, there was Hollywood melodrama and exaggeration—but he also found himself unexpectedly captivated by Mr. Keating, the teacher in the film. Mr. Keating reminded James of his algebra teacher, Mrs. Schneider, who had been one of the most beloved teachers at his high school. He realized that loving one's subject made a huge difference in a teacher's effectiveness. What made a truly great teacher was not just the techniques they used, but *how* they used them. Mr. Keating didn't just teach poetry, he made it come alive. He was impassioned by poetry, and his passion was contagious.

James was inspired. He wanted to have the kind of impact on his students that Mr. Keating and his former math teacher had on theirs. He wanted his students to love literature and poetry. And he wanted to learn how he could make that happen. The next day he returned to his methods class with a host of new questions swirling around in his head: *Would I enjoy this method if a teacher used it on me? If not, could I modify it to be genuinely engaging to students? Does the method fit who I want to be in the classroom? Or should I throw it out altogether?*

There was just one problem. James was an introvert, and he worried about whether he could be as compelling and engaging as Mr. Keating and Mrs. Schneider were. In fact, he was almost certain that he couldn't be. He invited a teacher friend to dinner one evening so he could confess his concerns. Luckily, his friend had some choice advice. He said that nearly all teachers have similar worries when they first start teaching; even Mr. Keating was an introvert outside the classroom. And he reminded James about the students' response to Mr. Keating on the first day of class. They seemed confused and put off, and they called his class "weird" and "spooky" when it was over. The difference between Mr. Keating and most teachers, his friend pointed out, is that Mr. Keating had the courage to risk seeming ridiculous.

This advice was a breakthrough moment for James. He resolved to try to show students his passion for literature in the hopes of igniting their passion for it too. If he failed, then so be it. Importantly, he didn't envision behaving like Mr. Keating. He wanted to find his own persona and not merely imitate someone else's. Nevertheless, like Mr. Keating, James wanted to communicate that literature could be deeply important to students' lives—not to help them find a better job or get into a good college, but because it could profoundly enrich their experience of the world. He genuinely believed that the images and ideas in novels, narratives, poems, and plays could inspire students to see beauty in the world and goodness in human interactions. He decided to let this understanding of literature govern how he would structure his class.

After being hired by a local high school, James immediately set to work on a plan for inspiring his students. First, he wanted to communicate that important books and ideas call for continual human discussion. He moved all his desks into a double horseshoe shape with the open end facing the chalkboard. This configuration promoted class discussion. But because some of his classes had as many as 40 students, he had to reconfigure his desks several times to get them all to fit. He finally succeeded, placing the desks so close together that students had to turn sideways to walk between them.

Next, he carefully chose what he would put on his walls.

He pictured a typical English classroom with quotes from celebrities or sports icons about the importance of reading. That wouldn't communicate the seriousness of his mission. He didn't want anything to distract students from the enduring ideas they would be discussing in his class. He decided to find some inexpensive landscapes, still lifes, and portraits. He visited local libraries and thrift stores and found several suitable prints that cost next to nothing. He arranged them as if his classroom were a small art gallery. When students looked up from their readings and assignments, they would experience inspiring images and ideas, just like in their texts. He also used lamps around the room rather than overhead lighting. This would communicate that his classroom was much more than a learning context. It was a place for students to come together to enjoy each other's company and discuss ideas with other living human beings.

Then James thought about what he would do on the first day of school. He knew classes would be dramatically shortened due to welcome-back assemblies and other events, so he'd only have a short time to make the first day count. He wanted his students to feel like something was unique about his class.

James decided to ignore the students as they walked in the classroom. He acted as if he was typing something on his desk computer and never looked up once as they found their seats. All the while, James never made eye contact with them and kept typing. Naturally, many of the students sat down with their friends and started talking; some sat silently; others surreptitiously looked at their phones. As soon as the bell rang, James silently, and somewhat mysteriously, walked to the door, closed it, strode to the chalkboard, and wrote the following words:

> Human beings are born free;
> and everywhere they are in chains.

After dotting the period with some extra force, James wheeled to face his students, "Is this a true statement?" At first, the students stared in silence as he looked around the room for raised hands. He then asked the question again and waited there patiently.

Finally, a student raised her hand. "Yes," she stated simply. Smiling, James remarked, "See how easy that was; now, what about someone else?" Another student raised his hand and said, "I agree." James said, "Excellent! How many other people agree?" Several students raised their hands. "Okay, good, now we are getting somewhere! But now the question is, *Why* do you think it is true? What evidence can you offer? Because when I look at my hand and your hands, I don't see any chains."

This question kicked off a back-and-forth with the students about what it means to be free and what it means to be in chains. James rehearsed how this would go, and when he executed it, he displayed a degree of passion and energy that even surprised himself. As each student answered, he paced around the classroom, demanding further explanations and asking for more and more answers. He varied his responses to questions, sometimes stroking his chin in thoughtful reflection and at other times nodding his head vigorously and pacing more quickly when the answers were on point. Many students were becoming visibly animated. They answered with more energy. They also laughed at his humorous asides, and exclamations of "Aha!" or "What on earth?! How can that be?" While not every student in his class of 35 responded, he could tell that he had everyone's attention. Not a single student was distracted, inattentive, or talking with his or her neighbor. James sometimes moved in close and whispered. Other times he clapped his hands together and said, "Oh, that is good…but what else?" This continued for the entirety of the shortened class as James led them to consider what it actually means to be free or in chains.

Just before the class ended and without breaking out of his persona, he began to take attendance. He quickly but forcefully called out their names while still pacing around the room. When the bell rang, all he said was that he would see the class tomorrow. He never once introduced himself to the class or even mentioned that they were going to discuss literature. For all the students knew, they might have been in a history or philosophy class.

The next day, James continued to engage the students in dramatic fashion. He began class by telling his students that this would be the hardest class they would take that year. In fact, many of the texts they would read were so hard that they were usually only taught in college. But he told them that he knew they were smart enough to handle them. He then (finally) introduced himself and told them the name of the class.

James continued by talking about *why* they would be reading such difficult texts. His reasoning was simple. Their readings were some of the most important texts ever written. But they were important not because they are classics, James emphasized, but because they can help students reach their highest potential as human beings. James referred to this task as "becoming more fully human." The point of the class would be to become fuller humans: to develop their rational, imaginative, and emotional faculties—qualities which distinguish human beings from other animals and make them who they are.

Many of James's students were reeling after these first two days, but he did not let up. He maintained his persona, which combined intense seriousness with dry, but witty humor. Within two weeks, he could tell that most of his students were significantly engaged in the classroom, and many even expressed their appreciation of the way he conducted class.

## *Understanding James' Hook*

James made several important decisions that made for a successful *Hook*.

First, James **started with the small things**. He recognized that the arrangement of desks, his choice of classroom lighting, and his wall decor all played an integral part in engaging his students. These things created an atmosphere in the classroom that activated students' imaginations and focused their attention on what he was saying and doing. The effect of this atmosphere was to shape—subtly, even imperceptibly—students' thoughts and feelings about literature from the moment they walked in the room. It also put James in the right frame of mind; his intentional decisions down to the slightest detail primed him for the rest of the *Hook*.

Second, James **did something unexpected**. In fact he defied their expectations in several ways: He completely ignored the students when they entered the classroom. Then he silently got up, closed the door, wrote a provocative quotation on the board, and launched into a Socratic discussion of its implications. Typically teachers introduce themselves in the first moments of class, take attendance, explain the nuts and bolts of the course, and introduce some of the key topics. James's behavior was unexpected from the beginning to the end. James hoped the difference would spark students' curiosity and prepare them to develop a new relationship to literature.

Third, James **put his persona to use.** That is, he exhibited his passion for literature in ways that were uniquely his own. He intentionally raised his energy level and "prowled" around the classroom stroking his chin and nodding his head vigorously when students made good contributions. He used rapid fire questions to increase tension and participation, but he also gave students time to develop their own thoughts and ideas. At times he whispered, and at other times he spoke loudly. All this drew the students into the discussion and helped keep the focus on the content of the class.

Fourth, James **foreshadowed what was to come.** James's first class suggested that something important would be taking place in his class. He claimed that it would be the "hardest" course they'd ever taken. He hinted that there was something deeply significant about his subject, something that students wanted deep down. In particular, James suggested that literature cultivated distinctly human faculties that would help students lead meaningful and fulfilling lives.

Naturally, James' *Hook* did not fully convince students of the truth of these views, but it set the stage for later moments in the class when he would drive them home.

These four elements contributed to an effective *Hook* in James' high school English class. How might these elements look in a different instructional situation—in a science context, for example, and with younger students? The next teacher uses a *Hook* in just this kind of scenario.

## *The Hook in Action: Mariela's Middle School Science Class*

Mariela knew from an early age that she wanted to become a teacher—she just didn't know *what* she wanted to teach. She came from a disadvantaged background and attended several underfunded schools in her childhood. Many of her teachers seemed burned out or resigned to the poor conditions in these schools, and this made her determined to offer children like her a better, more hopeful education. As a senior in high school, she had a physics teacher who showed her the fascination and excitement of science. After graduation, she enrolled in a teacher training program with a high school physics track.

Mariela enjoyed her coursework immensely and was excited about the prospect of teaching. But shortly before she reached the end of her program, Mariela had an experience that dramatically changed her views about herself as an educator.

During the student teaching phase of her program, she started teaching physics at a local high school. She couldn't have been more excited—ever since her own high school physics class, she had felt a deep joy and wonder in studying science, particularly physics, and she wanted to communicate this feeling to her students. She decided to be enthusiastic, animated, and even joyful about her relationship to physics. She wanted to make physics come to life, just as her former teacher did for her.

There was one problem: She was 21 years old, and she looked even younger than that. Students simply didn't take her seriously. A handful of students realized that her enthusiasm was more than just a sign of her youth, but many others seemed put off by her enthusiasm. She got the feeling that they found it "corny." She wasn't entirely surprised at this reaction because she had read studies in her college classes that documented how female teachers were often not given the same level of respect as their male counterparts.

Discouraged and deflated, she spoke with her informal mentor, a professor who had previously been a K–12 teacher. Mariela asked her mentor how she could get her students to take her more seriously. Her mentor explained that there was no easy answer to that question, but she then went on to say, "There are some forms of enthusiasm that, though they fit our personality, do not fit our audience." She wondered whether this might be one of those cases. She asked Mariela if she had ever considered teaching middle school.

Mariela's first instinct was to reject this idea. She had always imagined herself teaching high school, and she was initially saddened by what seemed like the end of her dream. But then her mentor told her a story about her seventh-grade son. He and several of his friends often complained that their science classes were too easy or predictable. They rarely felt challenged and often felt bored by the unimaginative tasks and assignments. Any teacher who could raise the academic rigor of the middle school science classroom while also increasing the students' excitement about the subject matter could have a huge impact on students. Mariela's mentor claimed that based on her experiences with Mariela over the years, she believed that middle school students might be the best audience for Mariela's enthusiasm about science. In fact, she could imagine middle school students really connecting with that enthusiasm.

Somewhat unexpectedly, Mariela felt a weight lifting off her shoulders. If she really wanted to help young people discover the joy and wonder of science, maybe middle school would be the best place to do it. After a few days of thinking about it, she decided to start applying for middle school science jobs.

Mariela was hired as an eighth-grade science teacher in a middle school similar to the one she attended. The first thing Mariela did was to consider how the non-verbal aspects of her teaching could facilitate her students' interest in science. She thought about what she would wear. She wanted to let the students know that scientific ways of thinking played an essential role in her life. She decided she would wear a lab coat every day while at school. Mondays through Thursdays her lab coat would be white; on Fridays it would be tie-dyed. She also decided to wear her glasses to school and only wear contacts on the weekend. She felt the lab coat and glasses were symbolic of her commitment to science, even if they seemed a little cliché. Interestingly, the students never thought this outfit was a gimmick. To Mariela, the lab coat and glasses represented the enthusiasm she genuinely felt toward science. Unlike her high school students, her middle school students took this enthusiasm seriously. Admittedly, there were a few chuckles at the beginning of the year. But within a few days, the students had almost fully embraced the look. By Halloween, some students even wore lab coats for their costume, going trick-or-treating as their favorite scientist.

As intentional as she was about her dress, Mariela was equally intentional about small things that create the classroom environment. Unlike James, who could move his desks around, Mariela had lab tables that were attached to the floor. And nearly all the wall space was occupied by cabinets containing science equipment. Mariela was nonetheless determined to create a distinctive classroom experience, so she got creative.

First, she created individual name tents for each place at the lab tables. Rather than using students' actual names, she used the names of famous scientists: Jane Goodall, Albert Einstein, Marie Curie, Isaac Newton, and so on. When each student walked into class on the first day, Mariela stood at the door, asked them their name, and told them what their "science name" would be in class. Then she instructed them to make their way around the room and find their name tent. She did this with a straight face and asked them to have a seat. This allowed her to take attendance at the same time.

Not surprisingly, the students thought this was a bit odd. There were some sarcastic comments, but she simply ignored them. Once the bell rang, she closed the door and said, "Welcome to your laboratory, scientists. Please come up to my desk and grab a lab coat from the pile on the desk, put it on, and follow me." She had purchased a set of inexpensive lab coats that students would use and return each day.

After assembling everyone in the hallway, she walked her students out to the front of the school. She then divided the students into groups of three; gave each group a clipboard, pen, and piece of paper; and asked each group to walk to a designated tree. Their first task was to smell the tree bark and leaves. Then they were to discuss which food smelled most like the tree. Finally, they had to describe what aspects of the smell made them pick the food they did. Mariela instructed her students to make their notes as precise as possible, and to keep their notes and conversations private for the time being.

Unsurprisingly, this direction was followed by rampant giggling. But Mariela kept a straight face—more or less—the whole time. She couldn't help but smile as she watched the students sniffing the trees.

Once a group completed the analysis, Mariela called the rest of the class to gather around, smell the assigned tree, and determine whether they could smell the food selected by the group. The class then voted on which group seemed to be the most accurate. Mariela remained serious the whole time and, as much as possible, made sure the students were also taking the assignment seriously. Once the votes were tabulated and the winning team congratulated, they returned to the classroom. Mariela asked the students to hypothesize in their groups what the scientific purpose of the experiment was. Why in the world would smelling tree bark and comparing it to foods matter for science? After a few minutes of musing, she asked students to share their results with the whole class. Students' answers ranged from sarcastic to serious, from confused to insightful. In the end, Mariela welcomed all the different responses. She then explained that science wasn't just a subject in school, but a way of engaging with the world that should be just as exciting and joyful as it is diligent. What they were going to learn in her class was to see with fresh eyes—and smell with fresh noses, and sense with all their senses. "Most people wander through life and never really experience the incredible richness and wonder in the world because they don't think of themselves as scientists," she told them. "That won't be happening in this class." When they ran experiments, she said, they wouldn't just be exploring physical "facts," but discovering how fascinating the world becomes when they use the scientific method. Finally, she told her students that they would start the practice of seeing reality for what it really is.

On the second day of class, Mariela greeted her students by their scientific names. They smiled and seemed to take it in stride. After they sat down at their lab tables, she asked them why they thought she used scientific names for them. The students offered many answers, some humorous and some serious. In all of her classes, at least one student gave a version of the correct answer: "Based on what you said yesterday, you want us to think like scientists. By giving us the names of scientists, you're reminding us that we're supposed to think like scientists." Mariela would get excited at this point and go a step further. She told them that their laboratory classroom was going to be a special place where they would study scientific ideas away from all the distractions and drama of middle school. She hoped they would build new bonds of friendship, learning to support one another as they explored the fascinating world of chemistry, biology, and physics. "This won't be just another class," she said. "It will be a scientific *community*."

In the days following, Mariela continued to break conventions and get the students excited about science. She had high expectations and kept telling them that, in a matter of weeks, they would see things as they had never seen them before. She also made them call each other by their science names during class. It didn't take long for the students to start enjoying her class and engaging more deeply in the material.

## *Understanding Mariela's Hook*

As the reader may have noticed, Mariela employed variations of the same four elements that James used in his *Hook*.

First, like James, Mariela **started with the small things**. For example, she carefully considered the way her outward appearance could contribute to her *Hook*. She decided that wearing a lab coat and glasses to school every day would best communicate her relationship to science. She also assigned students names of famous scientists. Moreover, although she was unable to change the arrangement of her classroom space, she chose to alter where she held class on the first day. This decision suggested that science wasn't only done in a lab or a classroom; it was about the quality and depth of our interactions with the world.

Second, Mariela **did something unexpected**. Having the first class outdoors was obviously unexpected. But Mariela's students were also not expecting to don lab coats or to assume science names on the first day of class. The assignment to "smell trees" was additionally out of the ordinary, as was her insistence that they compare the smell to common food items. These unexpected moves set students up to start rethinking their attitudes and ideas about science.

Third, Mariela **put her persona to use**. For her, science was not merely about facts, but about seeing reality in ways that can be transformative. So she transformed her own appearance and exemplified a unique engagement with science phenomena. Beyond this, her decision to pursue middle school over high school teaching was also closely related to her teaching persona, although it is quite distant from her more direct instructional decisions. Mariela's irrepressible love for science, her age, the subjects she wanted to teach, her future goals as a teacher, and her ability to speak to her students all figured into this persona. Her mentor helped her see that this persona was likely best suited for a middle school audience.

Fourth, Mariela **foreshadowed what's to come**. She told her students that they would be shocked by the new perspectives they would gain in her class. Of course, this is not to say that all her students were completely hooked by Mariela's first few classes. But if nothing else, they sensed that this class was going to be different.

## *Planning a Successful Hook in Your Classroom*

How can teachers construct a convincing *Hook* in their own classrooms? As we have seen, the two examples above have several elements in common. We have distilled these elements below and developed several questions to guide teachers' lesson planning.

1. **START WITH THE SMALL THINGS**

The *Hook* is a set of intentional actions a teacher performs to get students' attention. Some of these actions are overt, like when Mariela decided to dress in a lab coat or to conduct class outdoors. Other actions will be more subtle, like James' choice to arrange the desks in a horseshoe shape, to use lamplight, and to hang artwork around the room. Students may not be fully aware of these components of the *Hook*, but these components are crucial for ensuring that its more overt aspects are maximally effective. Paying attention to the small things reminds teachers to be intentional about all aspects of their classroom space. Starting with the small things helps students to sense that their teacher is deliberately creating a certain kind of classroom experience, and they will want to know what comes next.

*Guiding questions for planning:*
→ What will I be wearing? How will I interact with my students in the first moments of the class?
→ How will I arrange the desks in my classroom? What will I have on my walls?
→ What kind of lighting will I use? What props might help communicate the goals of the class?

2. **DO SOMETHING UNEXPECTED.**

For a *Hook* to be successful, some of the teacher's actions should be unexpected. This does not mean that *Hooks* need to be extreme or bizarre. Even slight moments of surprise can have a great effect, like when James ignored his students when they came in the door, or when Mariela had students put on lab coats. Other examples might be when teachers stand in the middle of the rows instead of at the front of the class, or when they lower their voice to a whisper to communicate something important. They might also look out the window ponderingly or allow silences in the room to go longer than usual. These devices show students that this classroom is a different kind of place—one where they will be expected to do and think differently. At the same time, defying students' expectations just for shock value would entirely miss the point. *Hooks* are not for shock value. They are meant to connect to the goals and insights of the lesson, even if these connections are not immediately obvious to students.

*Guiding questions for planning:*

→ What will my initial moments be in the class? Will I introduce myself, write something on the board, ask a provocative question?

→ How will the first class be structured? How will it be different from the standard formula of introducing myself and going over the syllabus?

→ Have I rehearsed my unexpected behavior enough that I feel comfortable using it?

## 3. PUT YOUR PERSONA TO USE.

The glue that holds effective *Hooks* together is the teacher's persona. As we saw above, James and Mariela played up or down aspects of their normal personality to create a persona that could captivate students' attention. This is different from trying to be the "cool" or "fun" teacher. Successful personas can also include the "scary" teacher, the "nerdy" teacher, the "calm and relaxed" teacher, the "caring" teacher, the "charismatic" teacher, and so on. Students in James' class were reeling after the first few days. Some of Mariela's students were snickering at first. But in both cases, students eventually began to appreciate their teacher's persona. The fact is that nearly any persona can work if it is authentic in some way to the teacher and calibrated to their students' needs and personalities.

*Guiding questions for planning:*
- → What is the demographic makeup of my students? Do I have a sense of how I might be able to make them curious, perplexed, or excited?
- → What aspect of my personality can I bring forth, amplify, or diminish to engage students in this way?
- → Am I confident in my persona? If not, what do I need to do to overcome my insecurities? How might I increase my confidence by rehearsing?

## 4. FORESHADOW WHAT'S TO COME.

Effective *Hooks* create anticipation in students by foreshadowing the significance of the course or lesson. When a *Hook* is successful, students are excited to attend class the next day and look forward to what's going to happen. Teachers can create this kind of anticipation by saying things like, "You won't believe what I have in store for you in this course," or "This lesson is going to make you question everything," or "Before you thought one way; soon you will think very differently." We saw this kind of language in James' and Mariela's classrooms. These simple but bold statements can have tremendous effect. They create positive tension between the present moment and the ultimate goals of the course or lesson and prime students for the important shifts of perspective that occur in the *Pitch* and the *Awakening*.

*Guiding questions for planning:*
- → How can I allude to and build anticipation toward the content of the course?
- → What is particularly fascinating and exciting about my topic, subject matter, or subject as a whole that I could hint at?

## Troubleshooting the Hook

The four essentials just discussed provide guidance for successfully planning a *Hook* in upcoming lessons. But what should teachers do if they have already attempted a *Hook,* and it didn't go as planned? In our conversations with teachers, the following issues come up the most.

**TEACHER:** My *Hook* didn't work. What did I do wrong?

**RESPONSE**: Did you cover all four of the Hook essentials? Covering the essentials is a must for implementing effective *Hooks.* Did you rearrange your room or choose your mode of address carefully? If not, why not? Did you do something unexpected? If not, why not? Did you have a persona that connects to an authentic aspect of your personality? If not, why not? Did you foreshadow the fascinating next steps in store for the students? If not, why not? Finally, did you rehearse your *Hook* enough so that you felt comfortable with it, without memorizing it?

**TEACHER:** I covered all the essentials and I rehearsed several times. Yet my *Hook* still didn't work. This is a new class for me this year, and there are a few "difficult" students. Maybe that's why things didn't go as planned.

**RESPONSE:** Were you confident in the success of your *Hook*? *Hooks* take courage to execute in the classroom. They require teachers to say and do things that are often outside their comfort zone, especially when they are teaching a new class or have difficult students. After teachers begin regularly using *Hooks* in their classes, this feeling will (mostly) go away. But when teachers are first starting out, their courage may falter—even if they have planned a great *Hook*. This is one of the most common reasons that we have seen *Hooks* go wrong. Once a teacher plans a *Hook*, they should be confident about it—or at least pretend to be confident about it in front of their students. They should give their *Hook* their all, even if they are worried about its ultimate success. Often, their *Hook* is much better than they may think.

**TEACHER:** I had confidence in my *Hook* and was certain that it would work, but the students seemed confused, even uncomfortable, when I tried it out. They just weren't convinced.

**RESPONSE:** Are you sure that your *Hook* didn't work?

It's normal to worry about whether one's *Hook* was ineffective, over-the-top, or corny. Even successful *Hooks* often leave students bemused or bewildered. We have found that it often takes time for students to grow accustomed to teaching that defies their expectations or demands more of their engagement than is typical. Typically, students grow to trust their teachers' aims and intentions in the *Hook*. It is often best to maintain confidence in one's *Hook*, even if it doesn't fully land with students. However, there are occasions, like we saw with Mariela, when the teacher needs to reevaluate the types of students they are teaching and determine whether their *Hook* needs to be modified. To determine whether it is time to shift gears, the teacher needs to get feedback from the students. We will cover this in the next troubleshooting section.

**TEACHER:** I covered all the elements of the *Hook*; I was confident in my approach; I rehearsed it dutifully; and I stuck with it—but it still didn't work. My students were resistant, even hostile at times. What can I do?

**RESPONSE:** Go get feedback.

Every class is unique, as is every student. Getting to know the personalities of so many young people is one of the most rewarding aspects of teaching, but it is also one of the most challenging. Sometimes a *Hook* doesn't work as well as we would like because of the personal and interpersonal characteristics of a particular class. When this happens, we need to adjust our *Hook* to make it effective. But how do we discover what needs to be changed? The answer is simple: ask the students how the class is going, about what is working and not working. Make it an honest and open conversation. Teachers can do this with a full class, with individual conversations, or with small group assignments in which students are tasked with generating ideas for how to make the class better. This takes courage, but some of our best ideas about teaching have come from the minds of students rather than from pedagogy textbooks. Of course, this does not mean that the teacher should ask their students explicitly, "Did my *Hook* work?" They can, however, ask their students, "What was something that surprised you today?" or "What was something you wondered about when you left class yesterday?" This kind of indirect feedback often provides clues about what the students experienced.

# The Pitch

FOR STUDENTS TO BE engaged at the highest level, it's not enough for them to be *told* how significant the subject is. The most engaging classrooms enable students to *experience* the value of subject matter for themselves. By "value" we mean something more than appreciating the subject's usefulness or applicability. Typically, students already understand that their classes are necessary for graduation, career advancement or skill development. But they less often appreciate the wonder, beauty, or richness of school subjects in their own right.

The *Pitch* is a deliberate attempt to encourage this kind of appreciation of the course material. In the *Pitch*, teachers move beyond the attention-grabbing devices of the *Hook* and turn students' attention toward the aspects of their subjects that are deeply exciting or inspiring. The *Pitch* is founded on a faith that mathematics, social studies, English literature, and other school subjects are fascinating in themselves, if only students could come to see them as other than mere requirements. The *Pitch* is not an argument for the subject's "relevance," however. It is a demonstration of how subject matter can deeply enrich a human life.

The best way to understand the *Pitch* is to see it in action. Let's take a look at two teachers who employ several essential features of the *Pitch*: Jenn, a high school mathematics teacher, and Devin, a college philosophy professor. Both teachers were able to create effective instructional *Pitches* in spite of several initial challenges and setbacks.

## *The Pitch in Action: Jenn's High School Mathematics Class*

Jenn had always wanted to be a math teacher. Her dad was a math teacher, and he seemed to enjoy teaching math. Because Jenn was also very good at the subject, she thought that teaching math would be just as fulfilling for her as it had been for her dad. When she entered college and declared mathematics education as her major, she continued to feel confirmed in her career choice. She enjoyed her studies and took her education seriously, getting mostly As. By the time she reached her senior year, she felt prepared to teach math to high school students and looked forward to the opportunity.

Unfortunately, student teaching was much less exciting than she hoped it would be. She prepared her lessons conscientiously and was naturally skilled at explaining math concepts and ideas. But something seemed to be missing. She felt like her classes were just average. Students behaved and learned some math, but that was it—nothing really important ever happened. Her cooperating teacher told her that she thought Jenn was doing a great job and that she was going to be a good teacher. But Jenn herself was a bit bored by her classes. By the time she finished her student teaching, she seriously doubted whether she would enjoy teaching math for her career.

Not knowing what else to do, Jenn decided to look for jobs as a math teacher anyway. Her hope was that, if she were at a different school or taught a different grade level, perhaps she would enjoy teaching more.

Jenn was eventually hired by a local charter school to teach mostly upper-level math courses—something she was not able to do as a student teacher. She hoped that the added complexity and challenge would increase her enjoyment of teaching. And it did, but only slightly. She liked figuring out how to break down complex concepts like derivatives and integrals, sine and cosine, and explain them to students in simple and understandable terms. But once she had done so, she felt her stimulation wane. Added to this were all of the taxing professional pressures that she hadn't experienced as a student teacher: grading deadlines, annoying parents, behavioral issues, school shooter trainings. A few years in, Jenn found herself wondering yet again whether she had made the right career choice.

Serendipitously, a colleague from Jenn's math education cohort sent her an article about how teaching math, or any other subject, wasn't just about helping students to learn math concepts or achieve good grades. It is also about helping them to fall in love with mathematics. The author used the example of his high school math teacher who had a major impact on his appreciation of math. Her name was

Mrs. Smith, and she was obsessed with math. According to the author, entering Mrs. Smith's class was like stepping into "the Temple of Mathematics." She treated equations as "objects of reverence" and saw real beauty in the operations and ideas she taught. She would get visibly excited when she discussed paradoxes like division by zero, and this excitement was contagious. The author of the article claimed that he and his classmates were transformed by this teacher and her approach.

Reading through the article, Jenn could almost feel Mrs. Smith's passion for math leap off the page. For the first time ever, she really thought that math could be something more than just intellectually challenging. It could be inspiring; it could be captivating; it could even be elegant. Strangely, this feeling about math was familiar to her, yet also new and surprising. It was as if she had always believed these things about math while at the same time she was just discovering it. Either way, she realized this new experience was the key to what had been missing in her classes.

What inspired Jenn most about the article was not only that Mrs. Smith genuinely believed that math was beautiful and inspiring, but also that her students would come to find it beautiful and inspiring too. According to the article, Mrs. Smith didn't try to prove this to students. She tried to *show* it:

> I do not recall that Mrs. Smith used terms like *elegance, simplicity, paradox* or *power* to describe mathematics, but I do know that she showed us that these things were what motivated her about mathematics. These were words I acquired later for an experience to which she had pointed.

[...] Mrs. Smith was able to *show* us what mathematics contributed to her life. She was able to show us the beauty of a proof and the enticement of a puzzle. She exemplified [...] rigor and clarity. She was not satisfied until we got to the bottom of things.[18]

Jenn realized that she wanted her students to say these kinds of things about her and her class, the same thing the author was saying about Mrs. Smith. This meant she would need to make some serious changes to her teaching approach.

First, Jenn needed to deepen her new understanding of mathematics. Although she was convinced of the new approach, Jenn realized she would need to remind herself continually of its implications for her teaching. She had learned to go through the motions in her first few years of teaching, and her lessons had become mechanical. She had gotten used to telling students, "You'll need this for the test" and "This will be important for calculus" rather than pointing out why the topics were interesting and important in their own right. She vowed to leave these justifications behind. She was no longer going to teach math just because it was her job. She was going to teach math because math mattered to her life and to the lives of her students. She began to remind herself, "Math is profoundly enriching when it's understood correctly. Math is elegant and beautiful."

Second, she had to think differently about the planning and execution of her lessons. Previously, when starting a new lesson she would go to the relevant chapter in the textbook, look at the recommended outline and classroom activities, and create her PowerPoint slides. She knew she would have to change this. She would need to start her lesson plans thinking about the intrinsic elegance, simplicity, or power of the concepts to be taught. Sometimes this was thrillingly easy; other times she had to work at it. When she finally found some aspect or detail that fascinated her in the lesson, she became genuinely excited to teach it. She would immediately start to rehearse how she would explain the topic to her students. Of course, at times she imagined them chuckling at her enthusiasm, but she also believed they would, eventually, start to see what she meant—just like Mrs. Smith's students did.

She spent the summer on these two tasks—continually reminding herself of the beauty of mathematics and revamping her lesson plans. By the time school started she felt more excited about teaching than she ever had.

Her new year started well. Using Mrs. Smith as her inspiration, Jenn created a *Hook* in her precalculus class that was successful. After the first few days, the students seemed more interested in the class than they ever had before. By the end of the week, she was ready to start making her passion for math come alive for students.

Her first unit was on functions, which is where precalculus textbooks typically begin. Jenn asked her students to turn to the first chapter of their book. After they turned there, she asked them to break into groups and determine what was wrong with starting their precalculus class with functions. The students did this—albeit with some perplexity—and they came up with almost no plausible answers.

She told them that there was a specific reason they could not identify what was wrong with the chapter. "The reason is because you have never experienced math as it should be experienced. But don't worry. This is going to change for you. In this class, you are going to learn math for the first time." Jenn continued by saying that, before they could really understand functions and their fascinating behavior, they would need to close their textbooks and listen carefully.

Jenn told them that she knew, of course, the perception of math for many students, if not the majority. Math was boring; math was hard; math was something to be endured. She asked how many of her students would have said something similar. Most of her students raised their hands. She then asked the remaining students what they thought. Their answers ranged from "math is fun" to "math is interesting."

Jenn then told them that, in her class, students were no longer allowed to think that math was boring, nor even that math was interesting or fun. Math was so much more than that. It was fascinating—it was elegant—it was beautiful. "Just look at this," she said to her students, turning to the blackboard. A moment later, she had scribbled Euler's identity on the board:

$$e^{i\pi} + 1 = 0$$

As she turned to her students again, Jenn didn't exactly see a room of teenagers swooning over the formula. They looked incredulous or bemused, just as she hoped. She continued her speech. "Before, you thought of formulas like this as mysterious conglomerations of confusing symbols and imposing operations. And yet, this statement here is one of the most beautiful pieces of art ever conceived. It unites several of the most important and most fundamental mathematical ideas into one profound statement. In my class, we are not only going to learn what this formula means and how to stick numbers into it. I want to help you see it as beautiful, elegant, even inspiring. This might sound strange," she continued, "but I'm willing to make you a guarantee. By the end of the year, you will be just as convinced of the elegance of this formula, and the many others we will encounter, as I am."

Again, the students looked doubtful or humored by Jenn's guarantee. There were some snickers and sarcastic remarks about her having had too much coffee. It made sense to Jenn that her students wouldn't quite know what to do with this way of talking about math. Of course, she was realistic and didn't expect her guarantee to come true for *all* her students. But she did believe that she could have a meaningful impact.

And that's exactly what happened. After just a few days, some students started to imitate her excited exclamations about how elegant, beautiful, or exciting the math was. At first their imitations were somewhat ironic. They even became something of an inside joke for the class, and she was fine with that. She sensed that the jokes would gradually become real belief. Even though she enjoyed the joking and sarcasm, she made sure to tell students she was dead serious. During a demonstration or proof, she would whisper, "Isn't this amazing?" or "Do you feel the power of this formula?" or "So deep!"

During the next several weeks and months, Jenn's students still joked about math being elegant or beautiful, but she could tell that they took it more seriously. In fact, Jenn's guarantee became a central principle of her teaching. She would ask students to solve problems using different strategies and then discuss which solution was the most elegant. The students would then have to share which solution they chose and explain why it was more elegant in front of the class. The students caught on, and they would sometimes get passionate about why one solution was better than another. Eventually it became a source of pride for students when one or the other would use terms like "beauty" or "elegance" voluntarily during class. By the end of the year, not all of Jenn's students would have said that they loved math, but her experience in her classroom was significantly different from any other year she had taught. She felt it, and she knew her students felt it too.

Jenn continues to refer to the original article that inspired her new approach to teaching. She doubts whether her students consider her classroom a "Temple of Mathematics." But she knows they are engaging with math in a way she had not in high school or college. She recognizes that they see math differently, and it affects them in ways that make them eager to be in class.

## *Understanding Jenn's Pitch*

Jenn made several important decisions that laid the foundation for a successful *Pitch*

First, Jenn **expressed a passion for her subject.** Jenn's teaching was not initially imbued with passion and enthusiasm, of course. Jenn had to encounter someone who felt this way about the subject—Mrs. Smith—before she could begin to feel it too. In our experience, this is a common occurrence. Both new and experienced teachers often need guidance or inspiration from passionate role models in order to begin feeling passion for their own subjects and to have the courage to express it in front of students. Interestingly, the more Jenn shared these ideas and feelings with her students, the more her own passion for the subject grew.

Second, Jenn **highlighted the intrinsic value of her subject**. After reading about Mrs. Smith, Jenn began using terms like *beauty, elegance,* and *fascination* to describe mathematical terms and ideas. She wanted to communicate that math is something exciting on its own terms; it is intrinsically—and not just instrumentally—valuable. Jenn was honest with students on this point. She told them she had not always appreciated mathematics in this deeper way. But she made a guarantee to students that they would—slowly but surely—begin to feel this same kind of appreciation. And she supported this process by having students work in groups to defend why their answers were the most "elegant."

Third, Jenn **played up the mystery.** Jenn's "guarantee" was the most obvious way that she emphasized the mystery of where she was leading students. She promised them they would be inspired by math by the end of her class. Jenn knew that this guarantee was unlikely to succeed with some of her students. But she reasoned that its audacity would stimulate their interest and make students wonder if it could actually happen. She also subtly played up the mystery when she would lower her voice at times, suggesting that there was a secret about math that she and her students shared.

Fourth, Jenn **believed in her students' potential**. As Jenn began to see the value of math for herself, she also began to see her students in a new light. She ceased seeing them merely as people who needed to learn the content and began to recognize them as future lovers of math who understood the subject as vital to a flourishing life. She was so convinced of her students' abilities that she made them a "guarantee" that they would see math in this way. Not every teacher needs to make their belief in students' potential in such a dramatic way. However, figuring out ways to communicate this belief truly matters for increasing students' learning and engagement—it helps the students believe in themselves.

These four elements contributed to an effective *Pitch* in Jenn's high school Mathematics class. How might these elements look in a different instructional situation—in a college philosophy class, for example? The next teacher uses a *Pitch* in just this kind of scenario.

## *The Pitch in Action: Devin's College Philosophy Class*

When Devin was offered a full-time job teaching introductory philosophy courses at a small state college right out of his PhD program, he felt like he had won the lottery. The students he would be teaching needed to take these courses as part of their general education requirements for graduation. Although the vast majority of Devin's students wouldn't be philosophy majors, he felt up to the challenge.

His initial excitement was dampened, however, when he spoke to his dissertation advisor about the job offer. His advisor explained to him that teaching philosophy courses to non-philosophy majors would be very different from what he experienced in his college and graduate philosophy programs. The vast majority of his students would likely be resistant to philosophy, and many would find it tedious and difficult to understand. He advised Devin to think carefully about how to approach teaching these classes and to be prepared for unmotivated students.

Devin was slightly disappointed because he loved philosophy, and he realized he had always imagined teaching philosophy to people who loved it too. The advice was sobering, but he thought his advisor was probably right.

So Devin came up with a plan. His idea was to be as "accessible" to his students as possible. He wanted to show them he understood them—the long hours they were putting in, the pressure of studying for exams, their busy social lives. Devin decided to remind students regularly that he appreciated how difficult or abstract the reading was, and he might occasionally make a quip about the author's convoluted writing. His explanations of course concepts would be as straightforward as he could make them so that students could easily follow along. Toward the end of each class period, he planned to highlight the major takeaways on the board, particularly the ones students would need to remember for the exam. And he would tell them he knew philosophy was hard, but he would make sure everyone was set up to succeed.

When classes began, Devin's approach seemed to work well. He sensed that students found him down-to-earth and approachable, and they didn't appear stressed by his syllabus or the first few days of class. When he was fist-bumped by one of his students in the hallway, he was pretty sure he was on the right track.

During the second week of class, Devin began teaching Plato's *Republic*, one of his favorite texts. He opened in his usual way: He tried to come across as accessible and empathetic as possible. He started class talking about how dense the text was, even how tiresome the arguments were at times, and he made sure to ask students about their weekends and the upcoming midterms.

What happened next caught Devin off guard, however. Just after apologizing for the tedium of the text, a young woman raised her hand. With just a hint of defiance in her tone, the student declared, "I actually didn't find the text tedious at all." She said she liked the way Socrates weaved together all the examples and analogies for his arguments. Of course, it was hard to follow at times, but Socrates was such an intriguing character. He was a little annoying at times, but he was also fascinating and clever.

Some students began to murmur their assent, while others vocally disagreed. "I think Socrates is totally annoying. He's trying to intentionally trick his friends," said one student. Another retorted, "Yeah, but it's their fault that they can't see what he's doing!" As they debated whether Socrates was more annoying than clever, the class became more and more animated. The students were engaged in a way that both surprised and exhilarated Devin. He decided to run with their energy.

He said to them, "Maybe he is annoying, but what did you think about his refutation of the view that 'might makes right'?" A student nodded and said, "Yeah, I was going to bring that up. Whether he is annoying or not, he is totally right to argue against that view." Devin quickly responded, "Good. Let's turn to the end of the conversation to see what we think of Socrates' final argument."

From there, Devin had them analyze passages in small groups and explain what was being argued. He was blown away. Most of the students stayed totally engaged, and many of them—even those who were not philosophy majors—made astute observations about the text.

After the class period ended, Devin walked back to his office, amazed at the discussion he had just witnessed. It totally contradicted what his advisor had predicted, and what Devin had expected. These students weren't philosophy majors, but they were capable of enjoying philosophy as much as the majors did.

Devin was embarrassed and a little ashamed. He loved philosophy, and he had seen the value of it in his own life, but he led himself to believe that it couldn't be genuinely appreciated by the average student. He realized that he hadn't been giving his students or his discipline enough credit. He had believed that the best he could do was to help his students get through the course with as little frustration as possible. He wanted them to leave the course thinking he was a down-to-earth and reasonable teacher. But what he hadn't believed was that philosophy could be so intrinsically worthwhile that all his students could be moved by it.

This felt like a revelation. What he especially enjoyed about philosophy was discussing it with his fellow philosophy majors. He thought that they had been outliers, and that business majors, biology majors, or education majors couldn't or wouldn't appreciate the same types of discussions. But here he was teaching an introduction to philosophy course, and these same business, biology, and education majors were engaging in the material with as much passion as he had.

By the time he had arrived at his office, he decided that he was going to completely change his strategy. He was going to help his students love philosophy as much as he did. Rather than apologizing for how hard the texts were and focusing on explaining them in an accessible way, he was going to turn every class into a place of real discussion and debate. He still wanted to cultivate a close connection to his students and remain an accessible teacher, but he also wanted them to see that philosophy was worth investing in—beyond merely satisfying a general education requirement.

Devin spent two nights completely redoing his lesson plan for the following class. When he arrived at class two days later, he began the session by addressing the very mistake he had been making. Devin told students he had previously assumed that the best he could do was to help them make it through his course. While he had the best of intentions, he hadn't given them or given philosophy the respect they deserved. He was embarrassed to admit it, but it wasn't until he watched them debate about Socrates that he realized how much they could get out of philosophy. He said he was going to help them *love* philosophy as much as he did.

While giving this short confession, Devin realized that he had abandoned his standard casual stance at the front of class. He was moving in and out of the rows of desks, gesticulating with the *Republic* in hand. Devin noticed that his students were tracking him in a way they never had before.

His students' interest gave Devin further confidence. He began opening up about his own relationship to philosophy. What he really believed was that philosophy could change people's lives. In fact, it had changed his life. The first time he read the *Republic,* he hardly understood a word of it. But what he found so captivating was how Plato embedded his thoughts in a conversation between regular people without any philosophical jargon or formal arguments. He found that incredible. He told the class how the book had become like a bible to him—not because it gave final answers about how to live a fulfilling life, but because it posed the question in the first place. Engaging with Plato's *Republic* helped him see what philosophy was really all about: figuring out how to live the best kind of life together with the people we care about most. Philosophy may have a bad reputation for being abstract or complicated. But, in his view, it was one of the most important things in the world.

While his students were definitely intrigued by his remarks, he could see that they weren't completely convinced. He was prepared for this. He had the class divide into small groups for a longer class activity. The reading for the day involved the founding of Socrates' first ideal city, the so-called "City of Pigs." But before having students engage with what *Socrates* thought about the matter, Devin asked them to consider what *they* think belongs to a perfect society. Their task was to construct an ideal society that they thought was fully just. He encouraged them to think about what kinds of laws would be in place, what occupations would be found there, what institutions would be most prominent, and what activities would be most celebrated. He also asked them to give their city a name. As they began the exercise, Devin could sense a degree of excitement, and that excitement grew as the small groups began to exchange ideas.

After the time was over, Devin asked students what they had decided to call their societies. Unsurprisingly, they ranged from serious to silly—one group went with "Socrates Land," for example. Besides the names, Devin did not ask students to share what was actually involved in the societies they had founded. Instead, he said he wanted them to keep their own conceptions of justice in mind while they read about Socrates's ideal society. They would be missing the whole point of the text, Devin emphasized, if they just accepted at face value what Plato told them. That would be to remain *students*, but Plato wanted his students to be *philosophers*. This role switch is essential for understanding the text, Devin remarked, because Socrates is always trying to play mind tricks on them. Devin told them, "If you don't read and think like philosophers, you will make the very same blunders that Socrates' conversation partners do."

Devin could feel a greater degree of agency in these students than he had ever experienced in a class before. After a few class periods of similar framings and activities, Devin felt that his students were much more connected to him even though he stopped talking about weekend activities and exam stress. In fact, he came to realize that these conversations had often gotten in the way of constructing an effective *Hook* in the first moments of the class. Of course, he could tell that he sometimes missed the mark and lost his students a bit. But he kept getting better at finding the balance between speaking to students' current feelings and thoughts and encouraging them to consider new ones.

## *Understanding Devin's Pitch*

As the reader may have noticed, Devin employed variations of the same four elements that Jenn used in her *Pitch*.

First, Devin **expressed a passion for his subject.** After realizing the shortcomings of his prior teaching style, Devin decided to open up about his relationship to philosophy. He gave a short speech about his fascination with the subject and its role in a good life. To communicate this passion, he changed his stance from casual leaning on his desk at the front to enthusiastic movement through the room. Moreover, Devin's *Pitch* was effective in part because he used a special kind of story to express his passion. Devin shared a story of profound personal change that occurred in his relationship to the subject matter. Devin told students about when he first read the *Republic* and how it came to impact his own relationship to philosophy. Importantly, he did not make an objective case for his subject's relevance or importance; his appeal was personal.

Second, Devin **highlighted the intrinsic value of his subject.** Devin's *Pitch*, and even his expression of passion for philosophy, was not meant merely to reveal a personal idiosyncrasy of his character. Rather, his purpose was to communicate the deep value he sees in his subject. For this reason, he deemphasized the "uses" of studying philosophy—to get through the class, to get good grades, or to hone critical thinking skills—and focused on the subject's own power of fascination and inspiration. This focus on intrinsic value is essential for a *Pitch* to have the greatest influence on students. Not only does it grant the activities and assignments of the class a special significance; it prepares students for the breakthrough insights of the next framework step, the *Awakening.*

Third, Devin **played up the mystery.** The "mystery" here refers to the fact that students typically cannot experience the intrinsic value of subject matter for themselves. While Devin's students experienced an interest in Socrates' character and argument tactics, they had not yet fully understood what philosophy in general could contribute to their lives. Instead of seeing this as an obstacle, Devin used student questions, wonder, and doubt to create suspense and anticipation toward the end goals of his course.

Fourth, Devin **believed in students' potential**. Believing in students' potential is particularly important when they seem resistant to or uninterested in the subject matter, but it is always an essential part of the *Pitch*. Students need to be reassured that they will eventually be moved, inspired, or fascinated by course material—that they will come to see the intrinsic value of the subject. This was Devin's initial mistake. When he began his introductory philosophy class, he didn't actually believe his students could be inspired by the subject like he was. But he came to realize that the opposite was true—they could be, and even wanted to be, inspired.

## *Planning a Successful Pitch in Your Classroom*

How can teachers construct a convincing *Pitch*? Keep these four essentials in mind when planning your *Pitch*.

1. **EXPRESS A PASSION FOR THE SUBJECT.**
   The passion of the teacher is what bridges the teacher-directed *Hook* with the subject matter of the course. There are many ways teachers can express a passion for their subject, but one of the most effective ways is to tell stories about how their lives have been impacted and transformed by their subject. When teachers tell stories like this, students begin to wonder whether there might be more to the subject than they previously thought. Teachers can tell stories about how they first began to be inspired by the subject matter, how they struggled to understand the material when they were a student, or how they found ways to engage with the subject in their everyday lives.

   *Guiding questions for planning:*
   → What am I passionate about in my subject? Are there people or sources I can consult to strengthen my own connection to and passion for my subject?
   → How have I come to appreciate the subject? What stories can I tell of this development?
   → Can I relate these stories in a way that is humorous, inspiring, eerie, or emotive? What other sentiment might help to communicate these stories?

2. **HIGHLIGHT THE INTRINSIC VALUE OF THE SUBJECT.**
The goal of the *Pitch* is to convey a sense of the deep value and significance of the subject matter. That's why it is not enough for teachers to convey the subject's importance *for them*. When expressing their connection to the subject, teachers also need to show that the subject is worthy of passion in its own right—that their passion is not just an idiosyncrasy of their personality. Every subject is full of powerful and fascinating ideas that can inspire new ways of understanding the world. *The Pitch* gestures at the ways these new perspectives can enrich students' lives and expand their sense of what really matters.

*Guiding questions for planning:*
→ What is particularly fascinating, beautiful, inspiring, or enriching about my subject or the topic?
→ How can I refer to these aspects of the subject matter during the course of my lessons?

3. **PLAY UP THE MYSTERY.**
Even when teachers are able to tell students convincing stories about the deep value of their subjects, they will never be able to communicate this value completely—at least at earlier stages of students' development. This may seem like a downside, but it is actually the key motivating power of the *Pitch*. Put positively, a successful *Pitch* always carries an air of mystery. In essence, teachers are asking students to believe in something that they have not yet experienced, while at the same time suggesting

that focus and hard work will lead them there. Teachers can say things like, "I know you probably don't believe me now, but when we finish with this unit, your minds are going to be blown," or "As we will see, everything hinges on understanding this theorem," or "In order to grasp the importance of these passages, we have to become psychologists and get inside the character's mind."

*Guiding questions for planning:*

→ What can I say and do to suggest that there is something mysterious or wondrous about engaging with the subject matter?

→ How can I emphasize this wonder and mystery so that students' curiosity is piqued?

## 4. Believe in your students' potential.

The *Pitch* is rooted not only in a teacher's passion for their subject, but also in their belief that their students can feel this same passion. Of course, teachers do not need to be convinced that *every* student will, in fact, come to feel this way, or that the path will be easy. Rather, they believe that their students have the capacity to love what they are learning, and they commit to doing whatever they can to awaken this passion in students. This feature of the *Pitch* is essential. Even if students show resistance or openly doubt their teachers' appeals at first, deep down they want their teachers to believe that they can love what they learn. To foster this kind of belief in students, teachers can speak to colleagues about their students in positive ways and avoid complaining about them. They can keep their standards high and resist the temptation to lower them when students struggle or express doubt in their own abilities. And they can tell their students regularly how much they are capable of and how much they appreciate teaching them.

*Guiding questions for planning:*
- → Do I really believe that my students are capable of experiencing passion for my subject?
- → If not, what can I do to start believing it?
- → If so, how can I communicate this belief so that students can begin believing it themselves?

## *Troubleshooting the Pitch*

The four essentials just discussed provide guidance for successfully planning a *Pitch* in upcoming lessons. But what should teachers do if they have already attempted a *Pitch,* and it didn't go as planned? In our conversations with teachers, the following issues come up the most.

**TEACHER**: My *Pitch* didn't work. What did I do wrong?

**RESPONSE:** Did you cover all four of the *Pitch* essentials? Covering the essentials is a must for implementing an effective *Pitch.* Did you find a chance to express your passion for the subject? If not, why not? Did you highlight the intrinsically fascinating, inspiring or beautiful aspects of your subject, and did you do it in a way that evoked mystery? If not, why not? Did you tell students their hard work would pay off, or that the material would have special significance for them in the end? If not, why not? Did you really believe your students could succeed? If not, why not?

**TEACHER**: I covered all the essentials, and yet my *Pitch* still didn't work. Is it possible I don't feel enough passion for my subject? If so, what can I do?

**RESPONSE:** Seek out people, books, and activities that can inspire a passion for your subject.

The most important aspect of an effective *Pitch* is the teacher's genuine passion for the subject. Teachers who do not have this passion will be limited in their ability to create it in their students. Fortunately, teachers can develop and expand the enjoyment they take in their subjects, just as Jenn did. They can remind themselves that their subject matter has been a source of inspiration to many people in the past, and that it can become an inspiration for them too. This may take time, but as they think about the value of their subjects and express that value even before they fully appreciate it themselves, they will grow in their passion for it. Additionally, they can seek out people in their department or at other schools who seem to love their subject; they can visit former professors or other teachers who inspired them in the past; they can read books about the subject matter that bring the subject to life; they can participate in discussions or hands-on activities offered at local libraries, community colleges, or laboratories; they can attend cultural events on related topics; or they can visit museum exhibitions that take up aspects of their subject matter. Together, these things can help teachers develop a new appreciation of their subject that will increasingly transfer to students.

**TEACHER**: I genuinely have passion for my subject, but my students don't seem to be interested in my *Pitch*.

**RESPONSE:** Are you sure that your students aren't interested in your *Pitch*?

The first thing to keep in mind is that students will always be somewhat perplexed by your *Pitch*. This is the nature of this instructional step: The *Pitch* refers to feelings and insights that we believe students *can* have, but that they have not yet experienced. Indeed, students' confusion or even skepticism can help create an air of mystery. It is important for the teacher to keep assuring students that their perplexity will be rewarded.

**TEACHER**: At first, the students seemed interested in my *Pitch*, but as we got deeper into the material, they started to complain about how difficult it was.

**RESPONSE:** Have you built a culture of embracing struggle in your classroom?

As we mentioned in Chapter 2, an essential aspect of the four-step framework is building a classroom culture that embraces—and even celebrates—the value of overcoming difficulties. Creating this culture is essential for the *Pitch* to succeed. Teachers can begin to create this culture by telling students about their own initial struggles and how they were ultimately able to find a lasting interest and joy in the subject. Students are often surprised that their teachers struggled themselves, and hearing these stories can build a sense of community. But perhaps the most important approach is for the teacher to be partners with their students in the struggle. When teachers assign very difficult assignments but tell their students that they believe in them and will help them achieve success, students simultaneously feel cared for and challenged. This leads them to believe in themselves and believe that they can master the material. After all, the activities and pastimes that students will come to find most rewarding in life are often the ones that reveal their stimulating qualities over time.

**TEACHER**: I covered all the elements of the *Pitch;* I was confident in my approach, I rehearsed what I was going to say, and I have worked to create the right culture—but it still didn't work. My students seemed bored and merely went through the motions. What can I do?

**RESPONSE:** Go get feedback.

As we discussed while troubleshooting the *Hook*, each class and each student is unique, and sometimes we have to adjust our *Pitch* slightly to match the situation. We will occasionally have to ask our students how the class is going and what their experience of engaging with the subject matter has been. We can ask our students what is preventing them from seeing the value of the subject or from believing they will eventually see the value. In this way, they can guide teachers on what they might need to get to the next step. Having these kinds of frank discussion takes courage, but students genuinely appreciate the care and concern teachers show in doing so. Sometimes just asking them for feedback increases trust in the teacher in a way that significantly improves the success of the *Pitch*.

5

# The Awakening

WHEN TEACHERS successfully implement the *Hook* and the *Pitch*, their students are prepared for a special kind of insight into the value and meaning of subject matter. We call this insight the *Awakening*. When teachers create an *Awakening*, they build on the positive tension created in the previous framework steps and guide students toward an experience in which they recognize the power and wonder of the subject matter for themselves. Students discover that math, social studies, physics, or history are not just classes in a school day. They are genuinely fascinating and important subjects that can greatly enrich their experience of the world around them. When *Awakenings* occur, students will not only begin to take a deeper interest in the topics of the class and perform better on assignments; their lives outside the classroom will begin to change, potentially for many years to come.

This might seem to be a tall task for teachers. How do we know *Awakenings* can occur in the crowded classrooms and busy schedules of today's schools? How could we think that students could be so moved by course material? The answer is simple: Because we have seen these things happen in countless classrooms. In fact, many of us have experienced *Awakenings* ourselves. *Awakenings* are those moments when a teacher helps us see how learning can really matter for our lives. These are experiences that change us—sometimes just slightly, and sometimes dramatically.

The best way to understand the *Awakening* is to see it in action. Let's take a look at two teachers who employ several essential features of the *Awakening*: Mei, a college education professor, and Tariq, a high school physics teacher. Both teachers were able to create effective instructional *Awakenings* in their classrooms.

## *The Awakening in Action: Mei's College Education Class*

Mei is an experienced education professor who has a passion for uncovering unconscious biases regarding race and ethnicity in her pre-service teachers. She is particularly enthusiastic about showing students how these biases can shape their decisions in the classroom and undermine student growth. To accomplish this, she strategically constructs her lessons to culminate in moments of realization, in which students recognize the unjust or misguided character of their implicit prejudices and resolve to overcome them. For her, creating these moments is an art that takes tremendous forethought and practice.

Mei adopted this approach because she was dissatisfied

with the kinds of group discussions that she had experienced in her PhD program. Although Mei cherishes good discussions, she found the conversation in her classes to be at best meandering, and at worst a kind of pretentious banter that usually led nowhere.

At first, Mei imagined that she would enjoy the open-ended nature of these discussions. But as her doctoral program wore on, she became convinced that the directionless nature of her classes yielded very little in the way of genuine insight. The discussions didn't feel like anything urgent was at stake—it was mere intellectual ping-pong. While there may be a time and place for such discussion in the university, the classes she enjoyed most were ones in which she came away with a concrete insight into an issue related to real life.

Mei decided that when she taught her own graduate or undergraduate courses, she would do something different. She was fully committed to the discussion model as opposed to the lecture model, but she wanted the discussion to have an important end goal in mind.

In the final two years of writing her dissertation, Mei served as a part-time adjunct professor for several classes. In this role, she began to work on her approach to creating class discussions that dealt with issues of urgent and obvious significance for real life. By the time she gained full-time employment as an assistant professor, she had already developed skills that she would use during the following decade of her college teaching.

One of Mei's most powerful lessons in this regard comes during a class period of her educational justice course. Mei is deeply concerned about students' tendency to consider themselves immune to the prejudices, stereotypes, and racism that the educational theorists of the past often embodied. In her view, one of the greatest obstacles to educational justice is students' unwillingness to examine offensive views of the past because they assume they would never, nor could ever, share these views themselves.

Her own experience as a minority growing up in a largely white suburban school taught her otherwise. Many of her most painful experiences of prejudice came from people who were the quickest to condemn the racism of others. To help students see that they may have their own cultural blind spots and prejudices, she uses Aristotle's infamous, and frankly outrageous, defense of natural slavery. Her radical approach creates a deeply humbling *Awakening* in students that forcibly highlights their previously unrecognized propensity toward injustice.

In the text selection, Aristotle claims that certain people are born masters and others are born slaves. He argues that slaves are people who have an innate disposition to obey and cannot govern their own actions wisely. They are controlled by their bodily desires and do not have the capacity to guide themselves with reason. Aristotle argues that these individuals gain a certain amount of stability and safety if they have a master to provide guidance. Natural slaves should therefore submit to the direction of their master, since the master will take care of them. If they were free, the natural slaves would live a much more difficult and brutish life—a life controlled by appetitive desires rather than by reason.

Aristotle's theory is outrageous, and it might seem strange that a class entitled "Educational Justice" would even bother to discuss it. Yet, it is precisely because it is so outrageous that Mei teaches it. She allows her students to be lulled into thinking they are morally superior to Aristotle, since they all claim that they are totally opposed to viewing some students as inferior to others. The fact that they *feel* morally superior to Aristotle and express contempt and disdain about his morally backward philosophy plays exactly into her hands. She helps them see that, in fact, if they do not carefully guard themselves, their actions will implicitly support Aristotle's views. Ultimately, she attempts to reveal that they too have blind spots and prejudices toward others, and to feel a kind of constructive embarrassment at their own close-mindedness.

At the beginning of her class on Aristotle, Mei asked her students whether they agreed with his claim that slaves are better off being slaves than being free. Unsurprisingly, several students immediately chimed in and said that Aristotle was crazy, backward, or reprehensible. This is just what Mei planned. She posed the question like this because she wanted her students to clearly align their views *against* Aristotle. If she had asked, "Did you think Aristotle made some good points in his defense of natural slavery?" it would have muddied the waters. She wanted her students to think the matter is an open-and-shut case, and their feelings of outrage supported that reaction. She would reveal the troubling truth later.

Mei then announced the general trajectory of the class: "I am glad to hear you say you disagree with Aristotle. Slavery is a great evil and should be resisted whenever and wherever it occurs. And yet by the end of this class today, you will discover that you actually agree with Aristotle—you actually *do* think some people are inferior, and you agree that they should be governed by others. I'm going to prove that you think this." She did not say this in a condemnatory manner. Rather, her tone of voice suggested that proving the point would somehow make them better people. At this point, the class became completely silent. Mei was clearly very serious about her prediction, even if her students couldn't imagine how it could be true.

After this, through the use of small group and large group discussions, Mei helped her students understand the foundations of Aristotle's ideas about slavery. The students were supposed to arrive at the conclusions of the discussion themselves, without Mei telling them what they were supposed to take away. This was extremely important for student buy-in. If they believed that Mei was *forcing* them to believe something, it would be much less likely for them to experience an *Awakening*. She wanted her students to discover the insights themselves.

Mei helped her students make these discoveries by creating a dynamic discussion atmosphere in her classroom. When she asked simple questions, she would pose them to the entire class. For more difficult issues of interpretation, she had students get into small groups. There, students had only a small amount of time—one or two minutes, sometimes only thirty seconds—to deliberate, while Mei spurred them on with encouraging interjections, "Have you found the answer?" "Look carefully, it's subtle." "You can do it—concentrate!"

First, the students discussed Aristotle's idea that human beings are made up of body and soul. According to Aristotle, the body consists of nonrational instincts, desires, and passions. The soul, on the other hand, consists of reason, forethought, and reflection. Reason gives humans foresight and enables them to consider the implications of their actions. When human beings follow bodily desires and ignore reason, they often harm themselves and others. They follow whatever desire appeals to them at the moment and ignore their long-term needs or the needs of others.

As they discussed the difference between following whims and desires instead of following reason and forethought, students came up with many examples of why it would be bad for people to be governed only by their bodies. They talked about drug addicts, or children who only wanted candy for lunch, or animals who starved during the winter because they didn't store up enough food. In the end, students recognized that Aristotle was right on this point. It is bad for human beings when their passions and desires govern them in the absence of critical thinking.

Once the students had come to this conclusion, Mei led them to another key passage. Aristotle argues that individuals who do not have the capacity to use reason are better off when guided by people who do. This is true even if that means that the freedom of the former is limited. At first the students were doubtful, but the more they discussed it, the more they came to agree with Aristotle. One student, for instance, said, "Isn't this why adults don't let children live on their own and make their own rules?" "Another said, "Exactly! What if we let children do whatever they wanted? It would be total chaos, like *Lord of the Flies*." Mei's students came to the conclusion that because children have not yet developed the capacity to think critically and reason through their decisions, they would continually make mistakes—some of which could cost them their lives. Thus it is imperative for children to be guided by adults—for the children's sake.

After reaching this conclusion, the students really began to connect the dots. A female student observed, "Isn't this why we put people in jail who continually break laws and act selfishly—to protect themselves and others?" Perhaps, the student reasoned, it really is better for them to be guided by someone who could help them make wiser decisions.

This was a crucial development in the discussion so far. Mei pointed out—with some gravitas in her voice—that they had just arrived at the same conclusion as Aristotle: If slaves cannot reason for themselves, then they will be better off being guided by people who can reason for them: their masters.

At this point, the students were confused and a little shocked. They had initially believed that Aristotle was a completely bigoted and elitist philosopher who was only interested in oppressing slaves. But now they thought that perhaps his intentions were not as bad as they had assumed. But this led to the concerning possibility that, under some conditions, slavery might actually benefit the slave. Not surprisingly, the students were astonished.

At the peak of their confusion, Mei came to the rescue by drawing her students' attention to a short and easily overlooked passage at the end of the text. "We've missed something," Mei exclaimed. "Take a look at this." In this passage, Aristotle admits that he has a problem. He had decisively shown that *if slaves cannot reason on their own*, then they are better off ruled by a master. However, he had not actually proven that slaves *cannot* reason on their own. Mei then showed students that, in yet another often ignored passage, Aristotle himself admits that slaves often show as much ability to reason as non-slaves. And yet he never resolves this glaring issue in his theory.

Just at this moment, when the holes in Aristotle's case have started to reveal themselves, Mei points students to the key insight of the lesson.

Mei started by saying: "Up to now, Aristotle has made the compelling argument that if people are incapable of thinking critically for themselves, then they need people to think critically for them. You all saw the need for this in the case of children or criminals. So far, then, Aristotle makes perfect sense. The problem is that Aristotle makes a further claim that there are certain people, slaves, who are not capable of thinking for themselves. But what evidence has he provided? What evidence is there that slaves are born without the capacity to reason? There isn't any!"

She then went on to ask, "But why would he have thought this? How could he have been so blind? The reason is that when he looks at slaves in Athenian society, he sees a very limited ability to reason. The slaves just blindly follow their masters and don't actively think for themselves. But why is this not good evidence?! Discuss this in your groups."

In their groups almost all the students quickly came up with the correct answer: Slaves are not given an *education* that would teach them how to be governed by reason. Aristotle never proved that slaves don't have the capacity, as human beings, to reason. He only showed that, as slaves, they didn't *use* their reasoning abilities. Aristotle judged these individuals based on their *current behavior* rather than their *innate potential.* He didn't treat them with the dignity they deserved.

At first students were relieved to discover that Aristotle is wrong. Not surprisingly, they thought we should never assume that a person is incapable of reasoning; nor should they be controlled by another person. The students now allowed themselves to feel superior to Aristotle once again, since they were able to see this flawed assumption in his argument.

But before they congratulated themselves too much, Mei told her students that when they became teachers, they were going to encounter students every year who seemed incapable of using their own reason to govern their impulses and desires. She explained that these students will regularly, and often intentionally, disrupt their classes. In many cases these students will seem to know exactly what they are doing and take pleasure in the disruption. Mei admitted how disappointed, angry, and frustrated she was with these kinds of students when she was a high school teacher. And as the year progressed, she found that these students often became more difficult.

Here Mei shifted from her own story to her students: Mei said that it would likely be the same for them when they became teachers. Over time, it would become harder to believe in these difficult students and to resist disciplining them more and more harshly. They would be tempted to give their difficult students bad grades, send them to the principal's office, relegate them to detention, and see them as incorrigible problem cases rather than individuals with real potential.

The students nodded along to these points. Then Mei uttered the revelatory words: "If you do these things, you will be just like Aristotle."

"Even if you don't say it out loud," Mei continued, "you will start to think these kids *deserve* to be punished for their behavior and disciplined by people who force them keep the rules. You will say to yourself that you have given them so many chances, and yet they just don't care—they are willfully disobeying you, disrupting the class, and are just plain bad. Aristotle also gives up on slaves. He claims that they just don't learn fast enough, so they deserve to be slaves. You won't call your students slaves, but by giving up on them, you will be no better than Aristotle."

Her students were stunned. They were stunned because, having been students themselves, they remembered the kind of "bad students" Mei was talking about. They realized that they would likely become just as frustrated as Mei was and give the kids bad grades, send them to the principal's office, and so on. They saw for themselves that Mei was right—they did "agree" with Aristotle after all.

Mei ended her climactic speech and asked the students to discuss in small groups what they were going to do with the insight they had just experienced. She asked them to discuss how they could break this cycle for the students who were consistently reprimanded in class, given detention, or sent to the principal's office. Instead of improving their behavior, these measures often only deepened their feelings of alienation, loneliness, and resentment and led to even worse behavior. Mei asked them what they would do differently.

How could they help these students actually believe in themselves—believe that they could overcome their "bodily desires" and be "guided by reason?" These discussions yielded genuinely heartfelt commitments to treat these disruptive students differently—to believe in their students even if their students didn't believe in themselves.

## Understanding Mei's Awakening

Mei made several important decisions that laid the foundation for a successful *Awakening*.

First, Mei **unsettled students' assumptions**. Mei began her class by telling students they would agree with a thinker who endorsed natural slavery. This was troubling for students. They believed themselves to be against such an outrageous and unjust position, and in some sense they were. However, Mei's point was that her students harbored implicit prejudices and biases that are liable to come out when they confront difficulty or resistance in their future classrooms. As a result, Mei's students realized that if they did not develop a plan of action for helping their most at-risk students, they might end up failing to uphold educational justice.

Second, Mei **engaged their emotions**. At first, Mei allowed her students to feel angry at Aristotle for his unjust beliefs and express their concerns. When Mei showed that they agreed with the thinker in some regards, they were shocked and confused. This was not meant to discourage or outrage her students, but to cultivate the desire to do right by at-risk students. Mei communicated this intention in the ways she framed the goals of the lesson, and especially in leading her students to the cathartic conclusion that Aristotle was indeed wrong—just not for reasons they expected. In doing so, Mei created positive tension in the classroom that was made up of confusion, surprise, disbelief, curiosity, defensiveness, but also trust.

Third, Mei **created a breakthrough insight**. Mei had a clear vision of the perspective shift she hoped to produce in her students. Mei wanted her students to recognize how difficult it can be to avoid making biased and unjust assumptions about difficult students. She revealed that some of the most common responses to misbehavior and difficulty in the classroom were grounded in such assumptions, and that truly just educators cannot allow themselves to be guided by them. Mei had a well-designed plan to help them arrive at this result, and she carefully progressed through each step of the plan.

Fourth, Mei **made it real**. Mei used small and large group discussions to lead students to these key insights rather than employing a lecture model. Mei also encouraged students' personal and emotional connection to the subject matter, which contributed to the sense that these insights were their own. Mei ended the class by asking students to reflect on the ways they might teach differently in light of their *Awakening*, and this allowed them to develop a practical strategy for equitable teaching.

These four elements contributed to an effective *Awakening* in Mei's college education class. How might these elements look in a different instructional situation—in a high school physics context, for example? The next teacher uses an *Awakening* in just this kind of scenario.

## *The Awakening in Action: Tariq's High School Physics Class*

Tariq is an experienced high school physics teacher who is known throughout his school as someone who inspires admiration and respect in his students, but also some trepidation. Originally from Pakistan, Tariq immigrated to the United States after working as an engineer for several years. His family belonged to the lower rungs of Pakistani society, but he was able to work his way into the middle class by studying hard in school and becoming an engineer. He moved to the United States for political reasons and landed a lucrative job as an engineer. However, after a few years he became restless. He liked certain aspects of life as an engineer, but found it less fulfilling than he expected. As he reflected on himself and his time as an engineering student, he began to realize that his passion lay not so much in the practical application of engineering skills, but in the principles and foundations of the trade. He wondered if perhaps he should consider becoming a teacher.

This thought became stronger over time. Once the idea of becoming a teacher became more concrete, he realized he may have a lot to give to younger generations. He was grateful for the teachers that helped him improve his social standing in Pakistan, and he wanted to help his students in a similar way.

His first job landed him in a high school where the student demographics could not have been more different than the school he attended. His students were mostly upper-middle-class students, nearly all of whom were destined for college. Tariq was appalled to find that his students took for granted the education they were receiving and the luxurious lifestyle their parents afforded them. He could hardly believe how entitled many of his students acted and the laziness they showed toward their studies. Tariq realized that his students needed to learn a lot more than physics—they needed to learn how to care about something other than themselves. He made this part of his pedagogical mission. And the school where he started teaching is where he still teaches today.

Tariq decided to use his Pakistani upbringing as a part of his persona. He wanted to demand the very best of his students and show them how lucky they were to have access to a well-appointed school with well-trained teachers who cared about their educational development. He wanted them to see how much value and meaning they could discover in physics if they took their studies more seriously. Tariq began to let his students know quite clearly when they were falling short of his expectations. When he thought his students were being lazy, he liked to mutter *"Unbelievable!"* under his breath and shake his head with melodramatic disappointment. When they forgot something obvious or basic, he did the same, sometimes adding *"Insanity!"* just loud enough so that they could hear him. And when they turned in subpar work, he handed it back ungraded until they improved it.

Surprisingly, these seemingly derogatory comments didn't offend Tariq's students or hurt their feelings. He always managed to communicate that he said such things *because* he believed in them. If only they would try harder, they could exceed their expectations for themselves. His somewhat curmudgeonly persona combined with his passionate zeal for physics made the students want to impress him. And it set the stage for the kinds of insights and experiences he hoped to create in his classroom.

One example of such an experience occurred in a lesson Tariq taught in his 11th grade physics class. The topic was Newton's Second Law of Motion, and Tariq began class by expectantly asking students what this law is. Unsurprisingly, nobody knew, and this was part of his plan. After the class was silent for a while, he acted as if he was completely incredulous. "How can these students not know about this all-important physical principle?" he asked himself out loud, making sure to add an *"Unbelievable!"* under his breath.

Tariq's exclamation got some laughter, but he pushed onward. He told his students that they must know what the Second Law is. Not only so they wouldn't fail miserably on the AP exam next year—which they will do if they do not improve—but because it is fundamental to their understanding of how everything from neutron stars to soccer balls move through space. He said that the Second Law was even fundamental to whether they would be asked to the senior prom at the end of the year. "The problem is," he told his students, "I'm not going to tell you what it is."

Tariq explained his reasoning for keeping his students in the dark by asking whether his students thought Newton had the Second Law of Motion to lean on when he was observing the world. Tariq told them that Newton didn't have a textbook with all the physical laws written down for him. Newton couldn't rely on theories already explained in a book; he had to pay attention to nature. That was what made him an exceptional physicist. He examined things carefully. He had to ask difficult questions—"difficult," Tariq insisted, "because they have to do with familiar things that you take for granted because you're constantly sending texts and snaps to your girlfriends and boyfriends."

This slight at his students met with some ironic guffaws, but Tariq's next move really caught their attention. Tariq stated that the only thing he could do to help them in their "sorry state" was to "lock" them in the elevator. He led the class to the large, very old, rarely used, very jerky and smelly loading elevator in the school that is normally off limits. He brought several bathroom scales with him. He allowed students to bring notebooks, a stopwatch, and a calculator. No phones were allowed. His instruction was for half of the class to use the scale and pay attention to what happens to their weight when the elevator stops and starts, while the other half made a free-body diagram of the elevator in its various stages of movement. (Students learned how to draw these diagrams in Tariq's class the week before.) He gave them 20 minutes and told them that in that time they should find out what Newton's Second Law is. Then he stood silently across the hallway from the elevator with a stern look on his face.

Unsurprisingly, Tariq's students weren't able to come up with $F = ma$ (force equals mass times acceleration) at the core of Newton's Second Law. But they did recognize with some wonder what happened to their weight inside the elevator. It dropped when the elevator started downward and returned to normal a few moments later, and then increased again when coming to a halt. This was enough to pique students' curiosity, and they returned to the class intrigued, confused, and a bit rambunctious from the shenanigans in the elevator.

This is when Tariq began to reveal the connections that

explained the activity in the elevator. Tariq asked his students how many times they had been in an elevator, feeling awkward about not making eye contact instead of thinking about how the elevator can unveil some of the fundamental secrets of the world. "Now you have begun to unlock these secrets," he said. "You have gathered your data. Now you can begin to theorize."

Tariq then began a quick question-and-answer round in which he took in the students' observations from the activity, formalized them, and elicited all the concepts and variables necessary to derive the Second Law. He began by telling students that their measurements were much more than records of a joy ride through the forgotten corners of the school. He asked them, "What forces were acting upon you when you rode in the elevator? You don't just fall through the floor, right? What is the number one most important force that you need to survive an elevator ride?" Now his students answered: the upward force of the floor. He asked whether they had that force on the free-body diagram. If they didn't, he had them add it.

The next step was to figure out why their weight dropped. Tariq said, "Because this is an old elevator, the ride is not as smooth as a more modern one. But why? When the elevator starts downward, there is a jerk before the motor engages in the constant vertical motion. Did it feel a bit like you were falling to your doom?" Some students laughed and nodded. Tariq continued: "So what has happened to that force that was preserving your life?" It doesn't take long for a student to answer: It has decreased.

"If that force has decreased," Tariq asked, "what is

making them move downward? The same thing that made an apple plummet toward Newton's unfortunate head once loosed from the tree," he said. "It is gravity, and you were in momentary free fall. So why did the number on the scale decrease? What force did your weight measure?" Sharper students could see the parallel: scales measure the force that the Earth exerts *upward* on a body in light of its mass. So when the ground had been taken out beneath them, that number naturally decreased.

"Why would weight increase as the elevator slows down?" Tariq asked. The students had all they needed to answer this question, but Tariq still had work to do. A moment ago, their weight had returned to normal. But now they suddenly appeared heavier. What happened? The students answered that the force upward must have increased. "But what was the nature of *that* force?" Tariq wondered aloud. This was the key to everything that they had been doing, he said. Even though their weight was doing the opposite at the beginning of the ride, something similar was happening. Before they were speeding up, accelerating. Now they were slowing down. "What's a better term for 'slowing down'?" Tariq asked. A student eventually came up with "decelerating." Tariq pushed ahead with his line of inquiry: "And how do you express opposites in math?" *With a negative.* "So what was the common term in both situations?" *Acceleration.*

"Aha!" Tariq exclaimed. "Then, the force we feel is proportional to acceleration, whether positive or negative. Incredible! *This* is Newton's Second Law of Motion. You've done it," he said, still with a stern voice. And he wrote "Force = mass x acceleration" on the board. "Do you see the elegance of this statement? Do you see the indescribable beauty of how the cosmos works upon us?! *Unbelievable*, I tell you!" he said as he raised his hand above his head. "You must never forget this for the sake of physics—and for the sake of your souls!"

The students were humored but also a little moved by his passion. They wanted to believe him—to feel his passion for physics. But he was not finished. He told them that it wasn't just the laws of physics that were of supreme importance for their lives as students and people. It was all of the invisible forces that governed so many aspects of their lives.

Tariq pointed out that up to now, they had been going about their lives—riding elevators, driving cars, playing sports, or even just walking to class—almost completely oblivious to the countless pushes and pulls that their environments exert upon them. "We think *we* are the prime movers of our lives," he said, "but we are being moved. Science as a whole, and physics in particular, is about bringing to light forces that we do not see and understanding how they impact us." He then had the students think about what invisible forces were impacting them at that very moment. And he told them to be creative. "There are forces related to our physical environment, but also our social environment." He asked them to consider why some people succeed in life so easily while others fail; why some find good jobs and others end up in dead-end careers; why they get angry with their siblings or their parents, even if they don't want to; or why people they know are drawn to substances that decrease their well-being and health. Tariq then had his students get into groups and start making a list of these forces.

When Tariq brought students back from their group work,

he did not ask the students what they wrote down. Instead, he told them to keep the list they came up with; it was their "homework." He then recounted the story of his upbringing—how he became passionate about physics and wanted to become an engineer. Because people from his social class in Pakistan were only allowed trade jobs, he could not pursue his dream. He told his students about how hard he worked at school, and how the system attempted to govern his life trajectory like a natural law. Or, even more relevant to this lesson, there was always a negative force acting upon him, decelerating his progress.

Then Tariq shifted back to his students, helping them to take ownership of their newfound insight. If they wanted to be real physicists, he said, then they had to understand both the physical forces that govern how their bodies interact with the planet *Earth* and the social forces that govern how they interact with the human *world*. He asked them to think about how they might overcome the influences holding them back from their potential—whether they come from outside or from within. The list they'd just made was a starting point. It is important to understand why tides change and how radio waves travel unseen, but they also needed to find out why they lose their temper or become insecure. They need to learn about how friction influences the flight of projectiles, but also why they lack purpose or see school merely as a hurdle to jump on the path to financial security. Finally, they should study the principles of light diffraction, but also the reasons why they use substances they shouldn't or are influenced by other people's stereotypical desires and expectations even though it makes them stressed, anxious or downtrodden.

He told them that he wouldn't be standing here if he hadn't made the attempt to understand both of these kinds of forces himself, and that it was important for him to pass these insights on to others who may be in a situation similar to the one he was in.

## Understanding Tariq's Awakening

As the reader may have noticed, Tariq employed variations of the same four elements that Mei used in her *Awakening*.

First, Tariq **unsettled students' assumptions**. He told students that Newton's Second Law was not only an idea they had never considered before, but also one that governs whether they would be invited to the senior prom. This is not the customary way to talk about physics, and this is exactly what Tariq wanted the students to notice. He knew they had assumptions about physics and why the subject is important, and he wanted them to consider the possibility that physics could be more than they thought. Moreover, he talked about how elevators hold the "secrets of the world" and told them they would have to discover one of these secrets on their own. By making seemingly outrageous claims, Tariq is preparing students for the insights that emerged later in the class.

Second, Tariq **engaged their emotions**. Tariq interwove a variety of student emotions throughout his lesson. He used his curmudgeonly persona to produce mild intimidation along with mild amusement. He wanted his students to be a little scared of him, but also to find him a bit absurd. Doing this allowed him to challenge them without causing anxiety. At other times he waxed poetic as he discussed the elegance and beauty of physics, which caused students to feel his passion. Tariq also became more earnest when he shared his own experiences as a young man in Pakistan—especially his feeling of being at the mercy of institutions and practices he could not control. He encouraged students to feel empathy toward people who have lost control over their own lives and hope for themselves if they feel this loss of control personally.

Third, Tariq **created a breakthrough insight**. Tariq had a clear vision of how to help students grasp the Second Law and its role in explaining physical phenomena. He helped them gain this insight by putting them in a familiar situation and making them work it out for themselves. In this alone Tariq created a breakthrough insight that they would likely remember for the rest of their lives. But Tariq had an additional insight that he considered at least as important: he wanted students to see that thinking scientifically could help them discover and understand "invisible forces" at work in the social world as well. Students would have to reckon with these forces if they were going to lead freer and more flourishing lives.

Fourth, Tariq **made it real**. Tariq used various forms of instruction to create a multifaceted personal encounter with the course material. His lesson was partly about deriving and understanding Newton's Second Law. But as we have seen, his main message to students was the importance of being more observant of the world around them, seeing how some of the most important influences on their lives are invisible, and gaining control of these influences by means of close attention, reflection, and rational analysis. Tariq's approach was effective because his comments made at the beginning of this lesson placed his students on a path of inquiry that led to course content *and* their own lives. He wanted physics to become something more than a theoretical discipline that ended with mere intellectual understanding; he wanted his students to see the discipline as directly related to their "real lives.

## *Planning a Successful Awakening in Your Classroom*

How can teachers construct a convincing *Awakening*? Keep these four essentials in mind when planning your *Awakening*.

### 1. UNSETTLE STUDENTS' ASSUMPTIONS.

*Awakenings* are profound intellectual and emotional experiences that change the way students see themselves or the world. They occur when a student's former way of thinking and being in the world is revealed to be faulty or shortsighted. In order to set the stage for an *Awakening*, teachers need to unsettle students' assumptions; they need to cause at least some degree of doubt in students' minds about their previously held beliefs. Creating this doubt can be done in many different ways—some subtle, some less subtle—but it must always flow from the curiosity and growing trust created in the *Hook* and the *Pitch*. Teachers may tell students that something they have always believed will turn out to be the opposite by the end of class; they can tell a story about their lives that runs counter to what the students would have expected; or they can have students discuss their beliefs with one another and ask them to imagine alternative beliefs. In doing so, teachers should be careful not to state too early in the process where exactly they will be leading students. They need to maintain positive tension so that a breakthrough insight can occur.

*Guiding questions for planning:*

→ What assumptions, attitudes, values, or habitual ways of thinking might be standing in the way of my students' appreciation of the subject matter?

→ How might I call these manners of thinking and feeling into question in an intriguing way?

## 2. ENGAGE THEIR EMOTIONS.

When *Awakenings* unsettle students' prior assumptions, they are simultaneously performing a further crucial task: engaging students' emotions. *Awakenings* are most effective when students not only *see* the relevance or importance of the subject matter, but also *feel* personally connected to it. To establish this emotional connection, teachers must first experience the emotional connection themselves. Just like in the *Pitch*, the teacher must believe that the *Awakening* the students will have is essential to leading a meaningful life. When teachers genuinely believe in the importance of the *Awakening* they are trying to create, students are more likely to feel that a meaningful experience may be around the corner. Furthermore, teachers should try to create anticipation about the material that will lead to the *Awakening*. This happens in part through the unsettling of students' expectations, but it can also come from hints, allusions, or direct statements from the teacher about the *Awakening* the students will have. The teacher effectively communicates to students that something very important is happening or is about to happen in the class—that further engagement will lead to a crucial breakthrough.

*Guiding questions for planning:*

→ What is the nature of my own emotional connection to the subject matter? Do I truly feel and appreciate the importance of this lesson, or do I need to work on this before further planning?

→ What material might I use to create anticipation, tension, uncertainty, or suspense in class? Are there quotes, leading questions, instructional moves, clips, or stories that I could use to do so?

3. **CREATE A BREAKTHROUGH INSIGHT.**

The most important—and most difficult—aspect of the *Awakening* is successfully creating moments of insights in students. Creating these moments requires extremely careful planning. When creating an *Awakening*, the teacher must build the entire lesson with the moment of insight in mind. This is often called "backward design." From the very first, each stage in the lesson prepares students both intellectually and emotionally for the following stage. In the majority of cases, the moment of insight is most effective when the students are actively engaged in each step—meaning the teacher is not primarily using direct instruction. Of course, the teacher might punctuate each stage with comments or summaries of the progress they are making. But the main focus is for the students to experience the force of each stage for themselves. Finally, at the moment of insight, the teacher needs to give students time to absorb the experience. Teachers might have students write down their reaction to the insight, talk in pairs or groups about it, or think about ways they want to apply their insights in the future.

*Guiding questions for planning:*

→ What is the single most powerful insight to be gained from the subject matter for the day that I want to teach? How can engaging with this subject matter change students' lives—even if only in a small way?

→ How can I progressively lead students to recognize this new breakthrough insight or perspective? What other insights, perspectives, concepts, or facts will students need to have encountered before they can grasp the new insight when it is presented?

→ How can the breakthrough insight be introduced so that students see it as a product of their own thinking?

## 4. MAKE IT REAL.

Even though *Awakenings* of the most valuable kind are thoroughly planned and executed by the teacher, the students must recognize the breakthrough as, in some sense, their own. That is, it must seem *real* to them, as if it will have a concrete impact on their own individual lives. To ensure this happens, teachers have to show a bit of restraint. Their breakthrough insight takes students to the point where they can take one final mental step to begin seeing the world differently. But—this is crucial—teachers do not take this final step for students. As we indicated in the last section, teachers need to allow students to recognize the implications of what they have been learning for their own personal growth. Teachers may have students work out these implications in groups, in personal reflection phases, in applied settings, outdoors, or wherever else teachers think students can begin to make these connections.

*Guiding questions for planning:*
→ What concrete activities and experiences in students' everyday lives might be enriched by the *Awakening*?
→ How can I shift attention to these activities and experiences so that students think about how their *Awakening* affects their lives outside of school?

## *Troubleshooting the Awakening*

The four essentials just discussed provide guidance for successfully planning an *Awakening* in upcoming lessons. But what should teachers do if they have already attempted an *Awakening,* and it didn't go as planned? In our conversations with teachers, the following issues come up the most.

**TEACHER**: My *Awakening* didn't work. What did I do wrong?

**RESPONSE:** Did you cover all four of the *Awakening* essentials?

Covering the essentials is a must for implementing an effective *Awakening*. Did you unsettle the assumptions the students had about the context of the *Awakening*? If not, why not? Did you engage their emotions? If not, why not? Did you create a breakthrough insight? If not, why not? Did you make it real? If not, why not?

**TEACHER**: I covered all the essentials, and yet my *Awakening* still didn't work.

**RESPONSE**: Did you have a carefully prepared plan with a specific *Awakening* in mind?

All teaching requires a plan. But creating an *Awakening* requires a plan that is especially mindful of the intellectual and emotional factors at play in the classroom. *Awakenings* are a culmination of a series of steps that carefully build on one another—increasing students' curiosity and positive tension with each successive step. If teachers do not develop a careful plan, their instructional moves will seem disjointed and they will not culminate in the hoped-for breakthrough insight. Teachers need to ensure that each instructional step is closely coordinated with the intellectual and emotional states of their students, and closely connected to the steps that follow.

**TEACHER**: I covered all the essentials and I had a detailed plan, yet my *Awakening* still didn't work. Is it possible that my students' assumptions were *too* unsettled? They seemed to be really skeptical that I could change their mind about the topic, and there was no breakthrough insight.

**RESPONSE:** There is a difference between skepticism that creates curiosity and skepticism that creates contempt.

A successful *Awakening* follows upon successful *Hooks* and *Pitches*. If the imaginations of students have not been previously captured by a *Hook*, or their curiosity piqued by a *Pitch*, then it is extremely difficult to execute a successful *Awakening*. An effective *Hook* and *Pitch* generates trust in the teacher. If that trust is lacking, then students will likely find the unsettling of assumptions to be arrogant, naive, or foolish. They may even feel contemptuous at the teacher's belief that they will be able to convince students of something new or different. If a teacher *has* built sufficient trust through their *Hooks* and *Pitches*, then the situation is very different. Even if the students express skepticism about the unsettling of their assumptions, it will typically lack contempt and will often have an element of curiosity underneath. Teachers who have successfully *Hooked* and *Pitched* their students should not be fearful of this kind of skepticism. Usually if an *Awakening* doesn't work, it is not because of the unsettling of assumptions, as long as teachers have built sufficient trust.

**TEACHER:** Their assumptions seemed unsettled, and initially they even seemed curious about my claims, but as the lesson continued, they seemed to lose interest and become distracted. What happened?

**RESPONSE:** Did you remind students that a breakthrough insight was coming?

Once teachers have unsettled their assumptions by hinting

at a breakthrough insight, they need to continue to create interest and positive tension as the lesson develops. When teachers arouse students' curiosity by unsettling their assumptions, they need to communicate simultaneously that there is a deeper purpose behind this. The lesson should clearly move toward a culmination. This requires that the teacher occasionally provide opportunities for the students to "glimpse" where they are going. Sometimes this involves an explicit statement by the teacher. But at other times, students experience these glimpses in aspects of the lesson structure—for example, in a small group discussion about a topic in the lesson, or a short individual activity that reveals a new step on the way to the breakthrough insight.

**TEACHER**: I did hint at the breakthrough insight throughout the lesson, but when the moment came, students didn't seem to experience any insight.

**RESPONSE:** Are you sure they did not experience a breakthrough insight?

Knowing whether students had an *Awakening* is not always easy to determine. Of course, teachers could have students immediately discuss whether an insight occurred for them right afterward. But sometimes asking students to communicate their insights explicitly can, if not done carefully, act as a wet blanket. Momentous insights last longer if they are allowed to gestate before they are explicitly discussed. Sometimes the most profound experiences with pieces of music or works of art, for example, are remembered best if we are able to simply walk away and ponder them in our hearts, as it were. When a companion immediately asks what our impressions were, we are often at a loss for words, and if we try to express our experiences too quickly, the expression falls short and cheapens the experience. The same goes with the momentous insights we are trying to create in the *Awakening*. It is not always advisable to require students immediately to talk about their new perspectives or reactions to the material. To determine whether an *Awakening* occurred, teachers can subtly observe  facial expressions, body language, whispers with friends, and other similar types of clues. They will have to watch and listen. Even then, they may never be sure that an *Awakening* happened until long into the *Strengthening* phase. We will discuss this phase in the next chapter.

**TEACHER**: I watched students' reactions at the moment of insight and afterward. I carefully observed the body language of the students, and it seems clear to me that they did not have a momentous insight. What should I do?

**RESPONSE:** Go get feedback.

As we discussed while troubleshooting the previous steps, each class and each student is unique, and therefore we sometimes have to adjust how we execute our *Awakening*. To know how to adjust, it is essential to ask our students how the class with the desired insight went. Again, this is only useful if we have established trust with our students through our *Hooks*, *Pitches*, and *Awakenings*. With that trust established, students will be much more likely to explain what happened in the lesson and why the promised breakthrough didn't happen. As we have said before, these kinds of frank discussions take courage, but students genuinely appreciate the care and concern teachers show in doing so. Sometimes just asking students for feedback increases their trust in the teacher in a way that significantly improves the success of future *Awakenings*.

# 6

# The Strengthening

For Awakenings to take permanent hold in students' hearts and minds, students need to participate in a classroom culture that deepens and expands their newly gained insights. The insights of the *Awakening* generally fade quickly if they are not supported by tasks, activities, and an atmosphere of cooperation and comradery. Without these things, *Awakenings* become brief, albeit positive interruptions in the monotony of school, but ultimately fail to have an impact on students' perspectives or values.

For this reason, effective teachers apply an instructional element we call the *Strengthening*. In this phase, teachers find creative and engaging ways to deepen students' newfound perspectives, develop the skills necessary to support them, and hone their existing abilities. These allow students to try out the new ideas, perspectives, and self-concepts that they have encountered in the *Awakening* and further explore their promises and potential. The *Strengthening* is not just about applications, however. Its central aim is to solidify students' sense that the subjects they are studying in school are valuable in themselves and worthy of their time and attention.

The best way to understand the *Strengthening* is to see it in action. Let's take a look at two teachers who employ several essential features of the *Strengthening*: Margaret, a high school English teacher, and Terrell, a middle school social studies teacher. Both teachers were able to create effective instructional *Strengthenings* in their classrooms.

## *The Strengthening in Action: Margaret's High School English Class*

Margaret is a teacher who goes beyond just asking her students to read and analyze texts for their plot details and literary features. She asks them to read "as if their lives depended on it." Take for instance, her unit on *Hamlet*. She begins the unit by insisting that the reason we read *Hamlet* is not because it is a classic. We read it, she says, because Hamlet's dilemma is a universal human dilemma. At first, the students think this implausible, since Hamlet is a fictional character who lived in medieval Denmark. But Margaret helps them see that the deeper story in Hamlet is about the human tendency to be certain that we should do something, but then never to find the strength or courage to do it. She has the students read *Hamlet* to better understand themselves. What in their lives might prevent them from doing what they know they ought to do?

Margaret takes the same approach to the Romantic poets, to Kafka's *Metamorphosis*, to her writing assignments, and so forth. In each of these cases, she wants students to walk away from individual classes and larger units with a strong personal connection to the texts they discuss.

Margaret considers it essential for the success of her class that students develop a sense of intellectual community and shared endeavor. When students enter her class on the first day, she is aware that there is a host of behind-the-scenes friendships or animosities that are invisible to her. Students aren't just there as blank slates, ready to learn. Rather, Margaret realizes that some of their preeminent concerns are likely social in nature. She understands that one of the most important things she can do as a teacher is to help students overcome some of these issues and turn her class into a genuine community where students learn with and from each other—and not just *learn,* but also find a deepening appreciation for English and for one another. She wants students to see themselves as responsible for helping each other become their best selves.

Margaret has several different methods to deepen students' understanding of and commitment to the *Awakenings* they experience in her class. For example, her unit on Romantic poetry aims for at least two *Awakenings.* The first is a literary *Awakening* about how difficult it is to write excellent poetry. The second is an existential *Awakening* about how writing poetry is actually a communal undertaking in which the writer tries to help readers see the world *as it really is.*

She begins her Romantic poetry unit by asking her students how many of them look forward to reading poetry. This question often surprises them, and the answers she receives are almost invariably negative. Most students don't like poetry. When she asks them why, she gets comments about how "fluffy" it is, or how it is just about "expressing one's feelings." She responds by saying that her students are in luck because in her class poetry is about the least "fluffy" thing they could imagine. In her class, the poetry they read will *not* be "expressing feelings." In fact, she says, they will learn that poetry is the single hardest intellectual endeavor people have tried to do. She claims with complete seriousness—while all the time recognizing that her language is a bit exaggerated—that rocket science is easier; quantum mechanics is easier; neurosurgery is easier. Immediately her students become doubtful. Most assume that poetry just expresses subjective emotions in any way a person wants. But she tells them to wait and see—they will discover for themselves how hard it is.

She tells them that not only is poetry the hardest intellectual activity; it is also one of the most important creative endeavors ever thought of. When it is done well, it can help people see reality more clearly. She tells them that the best poetry opens people's eyes to see the wonder, terror, beauty, and mystery of the world. She claims that the kind of poetry they will learn in her class is not about expressing feelings— which can be done even by children without any education at all—but about helping people see truths that were formerly invisible to them.

From this introduction, Margaret leads her students to the two corresponding *Awakenings*. By the end of the unit, the majority of her students have come to see poetry in a whole new light and have a significant sense of its importance.

(This chapter is not about the full process that culminates

in these two *Awakenings* about poetry; rather, it is about what she does to help the insights gained in the *Awakenings* to become ingrained in the students' way of thinking.)

Having awakened her students to the profound difficulty of writing poetry and the way that poetry illuminates the world, she begins her first exercise: they must write a "perfect poem."

Margaret tells her students that it is now their job to experience for themselves both the difficulty of writing perfect poetry and the importance of helping each other see the world as it really is. She places them in partners (or, if there is an odd number of students, one group of three) and tells them that their task for the next three weeks will be to write a single poem that is no less than five lines and no more than sixteen lines. But here's the catch: The poem has to be an example of "perfect poetry." Every word must work together with every other word, as well as with the poem in its entirety. The purpose of the poem should be to communicate some aspect of the world they have found transformative in their lives—something inspiring, terrifying, beautifying, or mystifying—and it should do so *perfectly.*

Understandably, the students are daunted by this assignment. This is especially so when Margaret admits that she has never been able to write a perfect poem herself. She tells them she has tried and tried, but hasn't managed to achieve poetic perfection. Nonetheless, she believes they can do better than her, and she will be there to support them. She reminds them that in perfect poetry, the meaning of every word, the sound of every word, the syllabic meter of every word, the "feel" of every word, and the overall shape of the poem itself must all correspond and work together to illuminate the insight they are trying to communicate. This, she says, is what makes poetry the hardest intellectual endeavor. She is now expecting her high school students to produce poetry at this level.

As audacious as this assignment is, her students relish the challenge. The assignment comes six months into the class. During those six months, Margaret has built significant trust with her students through her *Hooks*, her *Pitches*, and previous *Awakenings*. They know that this assignment, while challenging, will cause them to become better thinkers, writers, and people. The students are glad she has placed such high expectations on them because they know it means she believes in them.

Margaret tells her students that they can consult dictionaries, other students, or the poetry they have read. They are also free to consult her, but she tells them that she will never recommend particular words. She will simply ask them questions to help clarify the kind of word they are looking for, or the kind of line or stanza they are trying to create. She reminds them that their colleagues in the class know just how difficult it is to write perfect poetry. Therefore, the assignment is an endeavor shared by everyone in the class, and each partner-group should do whatever they can to support the other partner-groups. In doing so, they are not only working with each other, but they are engaging in an activity that human beings have been trying to accomplish for millennia.

The energy in the room each day is palpable. Some groups look through dictionaries; others work with their heads together, trying to construct a particular line; yet others have moved over to another group and are asking them to read what they have written so far. Margaret walks around the room, encouraging some partners and goading others, all the while praising their efforts and also reminding them of the task's difficulty. Students cry out in mock complaints, "This is *impossible!*" as they bury their heads in the dictionary again. Others exclaim, "We found it! We found the word we've spent the last hour looking for!" Overall, there is a tremendous sense of comradery and excitement. This continues for the next couple of weeks.

As students begin to think they are close to finishing a draft, they are required to bring their poem to Margaret. She asks them why they chose particular words and why they decided on the rhythm of certain lines. If they cannot provide a satisfactory answer or if she believes there is a better way to express their ideas, she sends them back to the drawing board. Interestingly, they are almost never disappointed when that happens. Because of the trust she has built with them, they sense she is right. It makes them want to go back and improve.

In the end, the students present their finished poems to one another. After the class, as a surprise to the students Margaret prints each poem out on high quality paper, frames it, and hangs it on the classroom wall. When students come in the next day, they see their poems around the classroom. "Everyone's poetic aspirations should be honored," she says, "even if perfect poetry is still beyond our grasp."

Another strategy that Margaret uses to deepen students' insights gained through an *Awakening* is what she calls the "Great Bug Debate." For the final unit of the year, Margaret's students read Kafka's *Metamorphosis*. The story's protagonist,

Gregor, wakes up one morning to discover that he has turned into a giant insect. This story is a well known and terrifying existential vision of social alienation.

After completing the book, Margaret shows the students *About Schmidt,* a film about a man who, upon retirement from a mundane and meaningless job, discovers that his entire life is mundane and meaningless. This film serves as a step toward an *Awakening* about the dangers of being alienated from oneself and others by the choices we make.

Schmidt's wife—with whom he has no meaningful relationship, and for whom he does not seem to care deeply—dies just days after his retirement begins. Without his work or his wife to occupy his mind, he begins desperately trying to find meaningful connections with other people, but he fails time and time again.

Before showing the movie, Margaret tells the students that if they watch closely, they will see an uncanny resemblance between Gregor and Schmidt. They both feel completely alienated from themselves and others. Gregor's alienation stems from being an insect ... or does it? After the movie is over, she tells them that she is not sure Gregor actually turned into an insect. She suggests that it is entirely possible to read the *Metamorphosis* as an allegory about a person who suddenly discovers that he doesn't know who he is and doesn't have any real connections to people—just like Schmidt.

At first, the students are incredulous. Then she tells them that at least half of them will become believers after the next assignment. She then introduces the Great Bug Debate. Using extensive textual evidence, half of the class will attempt to prove that Gregor *is* a bug, and the other half will attempt to prove that Gregor is *not* a bug.

At first, the students who are supposed to prove Gregor is *not* a bug are disappointed because they think that they have the harder task. But as they reread and prepare for the debate, they start to notice uncanny moments when something happens to Gregor that makes more sense if he is *not* a bug. They become increasingly convinced that he is not an insect after all, but merely feels like an insect because of his sense of alienation. Meanwhile, the other group is becoming increasingly convinced that he *is* an insect. Working in subgroups within their larger groups, the students spend the next two weeks revisiting each line in each chapter of the book, preparing their cases.

The communal energy and excitement around this assignment is significant. Throughout the debate preparation, Margaret consults with both sides—but as with her poetry unit, she only asks questions to help them determine which direction they should take. Otherwise, the defense of their position is completely up to them. The sense of comradery is highest among the students within each group, but even between groups there is a good-natured rivalry that sometimes manifests as volleys of innocent and humorous "trash talking." The students take the assignment seriously but also enjoy the community-building that is occurring.

The excitement about the debate becomes so pronounced that students ask Margaret if they can invite friends or family to come to the event. It is a source of pride for them, and they want to share their accomplishments with others. By the day of the debate, the level at which each group understands the nuances of every section of the book is astonishing.

Like Margaret's poetry unit, the Great Bug Debate creates a tangible sense of community—in this case, around students' *Awakenings* about the *Metamorphosis*. Students take ownership of their theory about the book. To this day, she still gets emails from former students who tell her how meaningful the debate was and how they are still convinced that Gregor is or is not a bug. By working together, students developed a strong sense of agency to generate novel interpretations and defend them in a systematic way. This, in turn, increases their level of engagement.

## *Understanding Margaret's Strengthening*

Margaret made several important decisions that laid the foundation for a successful *Strengthening*.

First, Margaret **constructed activities that count**. To support her students' *Awakening* concerning the difficulty and existential significance of writing poetry, Margaret assigned a multiple-week project in which students were supposed to write "perfect poems." These poems should not only employ techniques and vocabulary that they had learned in class, but also communicate something personally important, profound, or beautiful that students had experienced. To strengthen her students' *Awakening* about finding meaning and real human connection in life, Margaret used a debate for which they prepared over several days. This encouraged students to look much more deeply at the intentions and overall message of the book they had read in class. The fact that students could also invite their friends to the final debate made the activity count all the more for them.

Second, Margaret **encouraged self-transformation**. Margaret insisted that, if they set their minds to it, her students could write perfect poetry and achieve something that they have never achieved before. Margaret explicitly told students that writing a perfect poem would help them become better versions of themselves. She communicated the same messages in the debate project. She encouraged students to reflect on their own personal connections to others and helped them to see themselves as a part of a community in which everyone grows.

Third, Margaret **let her students lead**. Margaret offered students some assistance with their poetry, but she did not provide any concrete suggestions. This allowed them to see the results of the activity as truly their own. Moreover, Margaret required students to champion one side of the Great Bug Debate with little help from her. Students could take ownership not only of the case they made for their position, but also of the course of the discussion as a whole.

Fourth, Margaret **invited her students into partnership**. In the perfect poetry assignment, Margaret admitted that she had never written a perfect poem and that she believed her students could do better than her. This created an atmosphere of mutual striving and foregrounded the common aspirations shared by Margaret and her students. Margaret commemorated their efforts by hanging up their poems on her wall. Margaret also used the Great Bug Debate to build comradery in her classroom, both between students and between her students and herself. It was a task that aroused their passion and excitement about literature—feelings that Margaret, too, had toward the texts she taught.

These four elements contributed to an effective *Strengthening* in Margaret's high school English class. How might these elements look in a different instructional situation—in a social studies context, for example, and with younger students? The next teacher uses a *Strengthening* in just this kind of scenario.

## *The Strengthening in Action: Terrell's Middle School Social Studies Class*

Terrell is one of the most beloved teachers in his middle school, where he has been teaching for almost ten years. Students can tell that he loves teaching, loves social studies, and loves his students. When Terrell was a middle school student himself, he had an English teacher who made him excited to come to class every day. This teacher treated the students as if they were adults and addressed them as Mr. or Ms. and their last name. She believed that if students were given more responsibility in the class, they would rise to the occasion. As a consequence, the teacher invited students to help her plan many of the classes, and she even had them teach class. Like the rest of the students, Terrell felt empowered by this teacher. She was one of the main reasons Terrell decided to become a teacher himself.

Terrell now has a similar reputation to his former teacher. He treats his own students like adults and invites them to participate in nearly every aspect of his class, besides grading.

When Terrell was an education major at a large state

school, he had a very clear vision of what kind of teacher he wanted to be. For the most part, he used his former teacher as his example. Unfortunately, he did not find his education courses to be very helpful in this regard; he was often unimpressed by their content. Many of the courses seemed to him either overly theoretical or simply flat. There was very little creative thinking about how to engage students in the classroom. In fact, he had one professor who told Terrell that his ideas about student involvement were unrealistic and unwise.

That is not to say that all Terrell's professors were unhelpful or unsympathetic to his ideas. A few were inspiring and even seemed to like how he planned to manage his classes. This included Terrell's college-appointed supervisor who supported him during his student teaching. But overall, he often felt like the professors themselves had unnecessarily low expectations of middle school students.

This was especially so of his cooperating teacher during his student teaching placement. He was assigned to a teacher who didn't seem to like teaching or his students very much. From Terrell's point of view, the teacher treated his vocation as a mechanical and frustrating job that had to be endured but not enjoyed. The teacher claimed to have high expectations for his students, but in reality his high expectations seemed more like excuses for why he didn't enjoy teaching. He often complained to Terrell about how entitled, disruptive, and apathetic his students were. The main reason the teacher's students acted this way, Terrell thought, was that they could tell their teacher didn't really cherish teaching them.

The contrast between Terrell's approach to teaching and

that of his cooperating teacher caused some conflict when Terrell took over the class. The cooperating teacher clearly felt threatened that students enjoyed having Terrell as a teacher. The cooperating teacher often subtly criticized Terrell's teaching methods, suggesting he pandered to students to get them to like him. Terrell was advised by his college supervisor to not rock the boat and to avoid employing some of the out-of-the-box methods that Terrell had seen his former middle school teacher use. Terrell quickly realized that he just needed to get through his student teaching and maintain the best possible relationship with his cooperating teacher.

It has been ten years since Terrell finished his student teaching, and he has never looked back. Once he had his own classroom, he was able to engage with his students in a way similar to his former middle school teacher.

Terrell does many things to *Hook* his students and *Pitch* social studies to them. He refers to them as young scholars and has high expectations for them. He loves social studies, and his *Awakenings* are meant to help students see the connection between historical and contemporary events in their lives. In particular, he creates *Awakenings* in which students see the ways common people—just as much as major political figures—are responsible for creating a healthy and flourishing country. It is normal for social studies classes to focus on large-scale events and national and international policies. He discusses these things, of course, but he also highlights the ways average citizens make a difference. For example, in one *Awakening,* he discusses the "Little Rock Nine" and emphasizes the role that courageous black and white citizens played in bringing comfort and strength to the nine students who desegregated Central High School in 1957. Of course, the federal government and airborne troopers played an essential role, but Terrell helps his students see how every person can and should play a part in making the world a more just place. Ultimately, he wants his students to see themselves as citizens who can make their communities better or worse depending on how they act. He constantly encourages them to grow as "people and citizens" for the sake of their family, their city, and their country.

Terrell takes these *Awakenings* seriously and employs several strategies to *Strengthen* them in students' hearts and minds. The first is to invite students to participate in the leadership of the class themselves. His goal for his students is that they be committed to full engagement in the classroom by the time they enter high school, even to the point of helping teachers succeed in their teaching. Terrell believes that many teachers often overlook the need to create a strong sense of responsibility for the entire class, and he attempts to make it an essential part of his classroom.

Terrell's process is elaborate because he places such a high value on what he calls "classroom citizenship." For example, Terrell meets with a group of five students every other week—the makeup of the group changes each month—to help brainstorm and plan what topics in the curriculum they should emphasize and what kinds of ideas and methods would most impact students. During these "citizen advisory groups," as he calls them, Terrell asks students everything from how they thought previous classes went, to what he could do to help students stay focused, to whether they think he should spend an extra day on ancient Greece or move on to ancient Rome, for example. Typically, the first few focus groups in the school year are on the quiet side because this is such a new and somewhat strange experience. They have seldom, if ever, had a teacher invite them to help them plan their classes. But as he *Hooks* students and *Awakenings* start to take place, they trust him more and they feel more empowered to give ideas.

In addition, Terrell works with the group to design and execute one short class lesson of their own. The students themselves will be the ones teaching the class. He reminds his students that growing as a citizen includes being willing to lead when called to do so. Leadership doesn't have to be at a grand scale—small-scale leadership is still leadership. He asks them to base their lesson on the ways history and culture affect their classmates, even if the historical events happened long ago. He helps them think through the *Awakenings* they had and then tries to help plan how to demonstrate this connection in the lesson they teach.

At first, just like with the advisory meetings, students are nervous about whether they can actually be successful in their teaching. He acknowledges their fears and assures them that they are natural. However, he also tells them that he knows they can do it and that they will even have fun. He has found that this combination of enthusiasm and confidence in their abilities helps calm their nerves. He also shares funny stories with them about his failings as a teacher—and gets them laughing at him. Then he tells them how laughing about his blunders reminds him that making mistakes is just part of the process.

Terrell provides his students with a great deal of support during the planning and preparation for their teaching. He is very hands-on, but he gives them as much freedom as he can to let them decide what to teach and what to focus on in that teaching. He also prepares the class to receive the teaching well. The point of having the students teach is not just for them to develop agency, but also to have their peers support and encourage them. Unsurprisingly, when the teaching happens, not everything goes well. But Terrell fosters a culture of comradery in which students voluntarily support each other, just as one might see on a middle school volleyball or basketball team. When mistakes happen, the other players remain positive and support one another. This is what Terrell aims for in his classes.

Another strategy Terrell uses is to meet with each student once a term to talk about their strengths and potential. One of the things he reminds students is that they continually need to grow as citizens and people. In these meetings, he begins by highlighting their academic strengths. He ensures that the strengths he highlights are meaningful and true; he doesn't praise them for strengths they don't actually have. Next he focuses on what he sees as their potential as citizens and people. For example, he might talk to a quiet student about a yet undiscovered leadership potential. He tells them that he sees them quietly offering some of the best insights or suggestions in class, even though other students hardly notice. But he tells them *he* notices and can't wait to see them grow in this area. Or he might talk with another student about their ability to empathize and put others' needs above their own. He praises these "soft skills" because they are ultimately going to make the world a better place. Terrell then offers each student one area of academic growth for the term. He tells them that by the time they meet next term he wants to hear about what successes and challenges they faced in pursuing this area of growth. He then asks each student to help him grow as a teacher by recommending one way he could improve.

## Understanding Terrell's Strengthening

As the reader may have noticed, Terrell employed variations of the same four elements that Margaret used in her *Strengthening*.

First, Terrell **constructed activities that count**. Terrell used two specific activities that engaged students in a dramatic manner: Implementing advisory groups and asking students to teach a lesson. Implementing advisory groups involved students in the content of the courses. Terrell made it clear that students were partially responsible for what happened in the classroom; they were not meant to simply show up and do what he ordered. And requiring advisory students to teach a lesson to the rest of the class demonstrated that these lessons "counted" a great deal, since these students were responsible for the learning of their peers.

Second, Terrell **encouraged self-transformation**. One of the ways Terrell encouraged self-transformation was by asking students to set goals for themselves. Rather than merely sharing what *his* views were about the students' strengths and weaknesses, he encouraged students to figure it out for themselves and to articulate a plan of action. He also encouraged self-growth by helping students overcome their fears and anxieties about teaching their lessons.

Third, Terrell **let his students lead**. Terrell's class is distinctive because he asks his students both to guide him in making curricular choices for the year and to teach their peers. Above we discussed how these are effective examples of creating activities that count. But, of course, they are equally effective as examples of how Terrell lets his students lead. They are, quite obviously, leading in a very direct way. At first glance, it might seem risky to ask middle school students to lead in such a direct way, but Terrell has found ways to make it work for his students.

Fourth, Terrell **invited his students into partnership**. Like Margaret, Terrell believes that his students are capable of partnering with him to increase their learning. Naturally, he doesn't consider them to be peers in a literal sense. He recognizes that he is still the one in control of his classes and the curricular decisions that should be made in them. But he believes that his students can help him see things he might not have otherwise seen. Although he is the teacher, he remains a learner. This attitude leads him to want to find multiple ways of inviting his students into partnership, as we have seen in the examples above. Additionally, Terrell referred to his students as "young scholars" and called them Mr. and Ms. in order to emphasize this dimension of his teaching.

## *Planning a Successful Strengthening in Your Classroom*

How can teachers construct a convincing *Strengthening*? Keep these four essentials in mind when planning your *Strengthening*.

1. **CONSTRUCT ACTIVITIES THAT COUNT.**

   For *Awakenings* to have lasting impact, teachers need to follow them up with concrete, interactive, and often hands-on activities. The *Strengthening* shows students what implications their newfound insights have beyond the lesson in which they occurred. This kind of application does not mean working only with examples from the "real world," though these can play a role in *Strengthening* activities. It means allowing students to engage with the content of their experience, exploring how it can further enrich their perspective, expand their skill set, and develop their sense of who they are and what they strive for. Teachers construct activities that count when they frame them as the next step in this growth. They say things like, "When you explore the economic roots of the slave trade in your groups, this will get you one step closer to becoming real historians," or "Working out this proof together isn't just some math activity; we're following in the footsteps of none other than Euclid."

   *Guiding questions for planning:*
   → What in-class tasks and activities can deepen and

extend the insights students have gained in their *Awakening*?

→ How can I connect the work students are doing to larger life goals and aspirations, like becoming writers, explorers, physicists, historians, and so forth?

## 2. ENCOURAGE SELF-TRANSFORMATION.

When students participate in class, they generally see themselves merely as students in a classroom. They are there to "do school" and be "learners." During the *Strengthening*, teachers encourage students to expand this view of themselves. They challenge students to see themselves as people of significant academic and personal agency who are gaining access to new and exciting forms of knowledge and experience. They are no longer students who are merely completing assignments required by a teacher, but individuals engaged in becoming their very best selves by means of the material. Teachers can encourage this shift of perspective by emphasizing the connection between what students learn in class and the self-transformation that the subject makes possible. Often this means making these transformations an explicit aspect of the *Strengthening* activities, as when teachers have students conduct personal assessments, develop their own ideas, and pursue their individual interests within the confines of the task at hand.

*Guiding questions for planning:*

→ How can I frame my *Strengthening* tasks and assignments so that students see them as opportunities to grow as people and lead a meaningful life?

→ What is the best way to talk about personal transformation as an aim of these tasks and assignments? Will students respond to explicit appeals, or should I bring in my own formative experiences?

**3. LET STUDENTS LEAD.**

The most effective *Strengthening* exercises have a high degree of student involvement. While the teacher will typically create and direct students' activities in the *Strengthening* phase, students should increasingly take ownership of the learning and growth that occurs in them. Often this means allowing students to become the teachers and facilitators of the very assignments they are completing. Teachers may have students plan a lesson or part of a lesson, organize a field trip, conduct interviews with each other, or generate assignments for themselves that they believe will advance their growth. The goal is that the community of learning in the classroom becomes self-sustaining even in the absence of direct teacher guidance and intervention.

*Guiding questions for planning:*

→ How can I get students involved in constructing and directing their *Strengthening* assignments?

→ What takeaways should come at the end of these assignments so that students can feel ownership over the results?

**4. INVITE YOUR STUDENTS INTO PARTNERSHIP.**

When *Strengthening* activities transfer leadership from the teacher to the student, they do not leave students alone in their agency. *Strengthening* activities are most successful when they take place in a culture of mutual support and inspiration between the students and the teacher. In this way, students increasingly see themselves as partners with the teacher in the shared pursuit of their best selves. In effect, the *Strengthening* helps students see that they have crossed a threshold where they now pursue goals and values similar to those of the teacher. This change in relationship allows teachers to further inspire and push their students. Students realize that if they continue to grow in their knowledge and understanding, they will increasingly become members of a community of scholars that includes their teacher and other inspiring individuals.

*Guiding questions for planning:*
- → What aspects of my class can benefit from student feedback or student direction?
- → How can I support students when they are given the reins?

## *Troubleshooting the Strengthening*

The four essentials just discussed provide guidance for successfully planning a *Strengthening* in upcoming lessons. But what should teachers do if they have already attempted a *Strengthening,* and it didn't go as planned? In our conversations with teachers, the following issues come up the most.

**TEACHER:** My *Strengthening* didn't work. What did I do wrong?

**RESPONSE:** Did you cover all four of the *Strengthening* essentials?
Covering the essentials is a must for implementing effective *Strengthenings*. Did you construct meaningful follow-up activities that supported or expanded what the students experienced in the *Awakening*? If not, why not? Did you encourage self-transformation by connecting their previous *Awakenings* with their potential higher selves? If not, why not? Did you give your students opportunities to lead in their own *Strengthening* activities? If not, why not? Did you invite students to partner with you as fellow members of an academic community? If not, why not?

**TEACHER:** I covered all the essentials, and yet my *Strengthening* still didn't work. It doesn't feel like a culture is forming. Rather, it feels like I am just giving assignments and they are going through the motions.

**RESPONSE:** Have you carefully thought through your activities and chosen ones that meaningfully connect with previous *Awakenings*?
Assigning activities related to *Awakenings* is essential to create a *Strengthening* culture. However, the kind of activities teachers choose and how they assign them also matters

a great deal. *Strengthening* assignments should connect to *Awakenings* in a deep and authentic way. A worksheet that superficially ties to a momentous insight will only decrease its momentousness. When students have a genuine *Awakening*, they want to be able to perform activities that reflect the importance of the insight. Therefore, it is essential for teachers to use tasks and assignments that closely connect to the *Awakening* in complex and challenging ways.

**TEACHER**: I chose my activities carefully and connected them to the *Awakenings*, and yet it doesn't seem like a culture of *Strengthening* is developing.

**RESPONSE:** Are you allowing your students to take ownership of their *Strengthening* by asking them to take the lead? In order for a *Strengthening* culture to develop, students should begin taking ownership of their own growth. The teacher remains important as an inspiration and guide, but the students are the ones who take the lead in establishing a mutually edifying community. It is important that the teacher trusts the students to take this leadership role. The students may not seem ready initially. But if the teacher continues to believe in them and continues to hold them to a high standard of leadership, the students will usually rise to the occasion. This is true even with students who have not been model learners. When teachers believe in them and ask them to participate in creating a *Strengthening* culture, they begin to believe in themselves and aspire to a higher standard.

**TEACHER**: I think that I have developed appropriate activities and have asked students to take a leadership role, yet I still feel like there is something missing in my classroom.

**RESPONSE:** Do your students see you as a true partner in learning?

In some ways, the ultimate goal of the four-step framework is for students to become so engaged in the subject that they feel they are partners with the teacher. The students come to class not as mere students anymore, but as fellow mathematicians, physicists, biologists, writers or, more generally, inquirers and investigators in common pursuit with the teacher. When this works, the classroom culture we have been discussing will become self-sustaining. In order to achieve this degree of common striving, the teacher has to communicate this goal to students and invite them into partnership explicitly and often.

**TEACHER:** I covered all these points, and still no luck. What can I do?

**RESPONSE:** Go get feedback.

As we discussed in the troubleshooting sections above, each class and each student is unique, and therefore we sometimes have to adjust our *Strengthening* to match the situation. Teachers will occasionally have to ask their students how well their *Strengthening* activities have helped them build community in the classroom. Teachers can also ask their students what they would need to solidify the insights of their *Awakenings*. In this way, students can guide teachers on what they might need to get to the next step. As mentioned, having these kinds of frank discussion takes some courage, but students genuinely appreciate the care and concern teachers show in doing so. Sometimes just asking students for feedback increases their trust in the teacher in a way that significantly improves the success of the *Strengthening*.

# All Four Steps in Action
# Katie's College Literature Class

NOW THAT WE HAVE seen examples of the four steps in isolation, it is time to see how the steps work together as a whole.

Katie teaches "English 100: Introduction to Composition and Literature" at a community college where she has been a professor for seven years. She loves teaching English 100—a required course—because it gives her the opportunity to demonstrate the profound significance of literature for students' lives. Her goal is for every student who leaves her class consider their experience a turning point in their relationship with literature.

The vast majority of her students are not English majors, and many of them are first generation students getting their associate's degree. This does not intimidate Katie—it actually invigorates her. She was a first-generation college student herself and began at a community college. While there, she discovered the impact that literature could have on a person's life. She came to her first English class barely knowing how to use a comma, but she left wanting to read as many books as she could get her hands on. She eventually received her master's degree in literature and now tries to create the same experience she had for her current students.

## *The Hook*

Katie's *Hook* begins as soon as students enter her classroom on the first day. She greets them warmly and chats casually as they take their seats. As soon as the class time begins, she hands out a half sheet of paper that has a quotation at the top from Ralph Waldo Emerson:

> Books are the best of things, well used—abused,
> among the worst. What is the right use? …
> They are for nothing but to inspire.

She asks students to reflect on this quote: first to try to understand what he means and then to decide whether they agree or disagree. They are to write their reasons for agreeing or disagreeing on the back of the paper and put their name on it. After they complete the task, she asks students to get into groups of three or four and discuss their answers. Their first job is to make sure they all agree on what the quotation means. Next, they each must share with their group why they agree or disagree with the quotation. If one or more of them disagree with another student in their group, they must try to persuade them why their opinion is correct. If they all agree, they have to work together to imagine what someone who disagreed with them would say.

Katie mills around the room, listening to their discussions

without offering her own thoughts. As Katie senses that a couple of groups are approaching the end of their conversation, she tells the rest of the groups that they have two minutes to finish. After two minutes, she calls time and first asks the groups to report on what they thought the quotation meant. After hearing from two or three groups, she then asks them if they managed to convince other members of their group. Usually this elicits slightly embarrassed smiles; some students admit that they were convinced, while other groups claim they couldn't come to a consensus. She then asks any group that was in immediate agreement with each other to outline what they thought someone who disagreed might say.

Katie lets the combination of the small group and large group discussion continue for as long as feels appropriate, and then she goes over the syllabus. Next, she describes their first homework assignment. The assignment is to find five students at the community college and ask them how many of the books they have read at college were "inspiring." They are to write their answers on the sheet of paper with the Emerson quotation and bring it to the next class. In addition to their findings about inspirational books, they need to submit to their course's online learning platform a 200-word narrative of what circumstances led them to the community college and what they hoped to achieve while there.

## The Pitch

On the second day of class, Katie asks her students to share the results of their interviews with one another. Nearly always, the results are the same: the vast majority of the students' interviewees report that almost none of the books they have read were inspiring. As she hears from more and more students, Katie acts out increasing dismay. She tells them that Emerson would be aghast at their findings and that he would view this lack of inspiration as the equivalent to an intellectual crime against humanity.

Katie then explains that there are two reasons why books are so uninspiring to today's students. The first is that contemporary academic culture is almost exclusively preoccupied with transmitting knowledge. For example, the point of biology classes is to help students learn facts about cells and organisms; the point of art history classes is to learn about classic art in each era of human history; the point of many literature courses is to learn theories of interpretation, or how to identify and understand the use of figurative language. It was almost as if college classes were designed to avoid inspiring their students at all.

Katie then moves to the second reason for the scarcity of inspiration in books today. She asks how many of her students were taking her class just to check off a requirement. Most raise their hands. Then she asks how many came to their first day of class expecting to be inspired. Few raise their hands. "You see," Katie continues in an exasperated tone, "we've stopped looking for, or even expecting to find inspiration in books. We read books just to pass the class or learn the facts."

Without transition, Katie launches directly into her own story about when she entered community college. At that point in her life, she couldn't care less about books. Then she took her first college English class, and she was transformed.

"In this class," she states, "we will be reading books

written exclusively by authors who wanted to uplift and inspire their readers. If you take this class seriously and open yourself up to the ideas we discuss, you may be just as transformed as I was." Katie tells them that she believes books ought to be "used well," just like Emerson wrote. She is going to help them see that books can and should inspire.

Katie continues by bringing up the narratives students submitted to the learning platform. Very few students had said they'd come to the community college in order to be inspired. But her hope was that, by the end of the semester, they would want to include "inspiration" in the list of things they wished for in their college experience. She acknowledges that there are many important reasons to attend college, and that the students were there for important reasons, but she wants those reasons to be coupled with a new reason. She wants her students to begin desiring, even expecting, to see the world with new eyes and to become better people through their engagements with literature.

## *The Awakening*

Using her *Hook* and *Pitch* to create interest and curiosity, Katie moves on to create *Awakenings* in her classes. She recognizes that creating an *Awakening* for every class is difficult, but she does her best. Even when an *Awakening* doesn't quite hit home, the setup for it often deepens or expands her *Pitch*.

One particular *Awakening* is based on a short story by Leo Tolstoy called "Master and Man." The story—which they begin in the second week of class—is about a landowning aristocrat, Vasili, and his peasant serf, Nikita, who become lost in a blizzard. In one sense, the story couldn't be further from the experience of the students. It is set in Russia in the late 1800s, and the main characters are people in a highly formalized class system that, on paper at least, does not exist in America. Yet, Katie tells the students that this is a story about them. They are human beings, and Tolstoy is inviting them to see humanity in a different light. He wants his readers to rethink what they value in the world and what constitutes genuine happiness.

Vasili is a seemingly mild-mannered merchant who is not exactly cruel to his serfs, but takes advantage of them when he can. He doesn't do this because he wants to exploit his serfs, but because he is a shrewd businessman. It is perfectly acceptable business practice, he thinks, to try to make as much money as possible so long as he does nothing illegal. If the peasants are taken advantage of in the process, that is simply because they lack business sense.

Vasili's servant, Nikita, is a generous, kind, forgiving, and courageous person; but he also struggles with alcoholism. He knows his master takes advantage of him. Yet Nikita does not have the business sense to know how to prevent it, so he accepts the meager allowance his master gives him. Nikita chooses not to become resentful towards Vasili and remains good-natured and kind to him, his family, and his animals.

As the story opens, the landowner Vasili decides to visit a neighbor who is selling some of his land. Vasili wants this land to increase his income. As Nikita prepares his horse and carriage for him, Vasili's wife begs him to take Nikita along, since a winter storm is brewing. Vasili assures her that he will be fine as he is dressed in warm, well-made clothing and knows his way about the forested countryside. But after her continued pleading, the landowner consents and asks Nikita to come with him. Nikita agrees and goes to his shack to say goodbye to his wife. She has Nikita put on his warmest clothes and boots, but they are ragged and not nearly as warm as Vasili's. Nevertheless, he remains cheerful as always.

As Vasili and Nikita travel into the storm, the master gets them hopelessly lost because he insists on taking the most direct route—a route that is infrequently traveled and has few road markers to guide them. When they end up arriving in the wrong town, a peasant family invites them into their home to warm themselves. The family begs them to stay the night because it has become dark and bitterly cold. But Vasili responds that he must make it to his neighbor so that he will not lose out on a bargain. The landowner confidently and repeatedly cites "business" as the decisive reason to act in one way versus the other. He is financially successful and believes that financial success is the same as happiness. Meanwhile, Nikita humbly seeks happiness in the simple things that surround him.

They soon leave the peasant home and, no surprise, the master gets them lost again—this time with dire consequences. They get stuck in a snowdrift, and the horse is too exhausted to go on. They cannot turn around and cannot move forward. They must spend the night outside, with the (slight) hope that they will survive. The internal monologues between the two men could not be more different. The aristocrat is agitated, then angry and bitter, and he blames his peasant for his misfortune, when in reality he is entirely to blame. Meanwhile the peasant is serene and experiences a connection with God and the certainty that God is with him, even in his seemingly inevitable death.

In Vasili's anger and desperation, he decides to detach his horse from the sled and ride it to safety. He is content to leave Nikita behind. Vasili does not make it far before the horse falls into a ditch and throws Vasili off its back. The horse manages to walk back to the sled. Vasili can do nothing  but follow the horse tracks, terrified of being left to die in the woods alone.

When Vasili reaches the sled, he experiences a sense of relief from the terror he had felt. He then discovers Nikita covered in snow and nearly dead. When he rouses Nikita, his servant barely murmurs, "Please forgive me." At that moment, something happens to Vasili. He realizes that he is warm because of his exertions and because of his thick fur coats. Almost inexplicably, he opens up his coats, lays down on top of his peasant, and wraps the coats around both of them. He says to Nikita, "Lie still and get warm." After a little time, Nikita, not really understanding what is happening, says, "It's comfortable, warm." Vasili responds, "There, you see, friend, I was going to perish. And you would have been frozen, and I should have…" He was going to go on, but the narrator tells us, "But again his jaws began to quiver and his eyes filled with tears, and he could say no more."

In this scene, Vasili has come to see something inexpressibly beautiful about life. He has encountered the simple humility and bravery of his servant in the midst of extreme stress, and this has made him realize the dignity common to all human beings. His terror of dying alone in the woods has transformed into a deep feeling of brotherhood and love.

Moreover, he recognizes now how much more important a human life is than the money he had so passionately sought. After several more moving reflections about the value of people and the simple things in life, he is himself on the point of death. Vasili says to himself, "Nikita is alive, so too am I alive!" Then the narrator tells us: "And he remembered his money, his shop, his house, the buying and selling, . . . and it was hard for him to understand why that man, called Vasili Brekhunov, had troubled himself with all those things with which he had been troubled." Then Vasili dies. Although Nikita loses a few toes to frostbite, Vasili's actions save Nikita's life.

The story is moving in its representation of fear, courage, sacrifice, and redemption. But what does it have to do with community college students in America? Katie helps her students see that it has everything to do with them.

Katie creates the *Awakening* by assigning the first half of the story (20 pages) for homework, right up to the point when Vasili and Nikita leave the peasant house. She tells them that after finishing the selection they must write a 500 to 2,000-word conclusion to the story. The only requirement is that it has to be in the same genre, meaning it cannot suddenly become a science fiction story in which aliens rescue the landowner and peasant from their demise. It must be realistic within the confines of the setting. She tells them that when they arrive in class she will ask for a few brave volunteers to read their conclusions aloud (assuming they are not much longer than 500 words).

When the next class begins, several volunteers read their conclusions. After hearing them, Katie asks if others want to summarize their endings. Finally, she polls the rest of the students about their conclusions to determine what percentage had a happy ending, a sad ending, or an ambiguous ending. At this point, she thanks all of them for doing the assignment and especially those who had the courage to read their conclusions aloud.

Next, she does something slightly unexpected. She stands up and, in a somewhat serious but warm way, reminds them of Emerson's quotation. "Books are the best of things, well used;… What is the right use? …They are for nothing but to inspire." She tells them that Tolstoy agrees with Emerson and has written "Master and Man" to inspire them. He wants them to think about what is important in life; he wants their vision to be transformed. This is why, she says, they must read the second half of the story together in class: to be uplifted as a community—that is, if Tolstoy can succeed at doing so. She tells them that she thinks he will succeed, and then she starts reading.

After finishing the story, Katie summarizes Tolstoy's hope for transformation in his readers. With a paradoxical combination of serious solemnity and energetic hope, she speaks frankly about the temptation in modern America to pursue the same material wealth that Vasili pursued; and just like Vasili, Americans assume that so long as they do not intentionally harm others, pursuing that wealth is an effective route to happiness. But the image Tolstoy presents is of a person who discovers that there are many more meaningful things to pursue in life—activities of inexpressible beauty and fulfillment. One does not need money to perform these activities, and money cannot buy the fulfillment that comes from them. Vasili doesn't learn this lesson until he is in the last moments of his life, but Tolstoy hopes that his readers will be awakened to the reality that one can begin to learn this lesson immediately—one need only begin to look around for opportunities to love and care for others.

After Katie summarizes her point, she asks students to discuss in small groups what prevents them from pursuing meaningful activities like loving and caring for others. Why is it that contemporary Americans are so consistently drawn to pursuing wealth as the most likely route to happiness?

After discussing this question in groups, Katie concludes this *Awakening* activity by reminding them of the answers they gave her on the second day of class about why they were attending college. Just before they leave the class, Katie asks them to consider what they might want to change about their answers having read "Master and Man," and how they can hold onto that insight as they progress in their college experience.

## *The Strengthening*

Katie employs many *Strengthening* activities in her course, just as she creates many *Awakening* experiences. In point of fact, every *Hook*, *Pitch,* and *Awakening* helps to strengthen students' commitment to learning. Every time teachers show care for their students, express their passion for their subjects, or lead students to dramatic insights, teachers are *Strengthening* their students. All these activities help to create a classroom culture in which students grow individually and collectively. However, relying on *Hooks, Pitches,* and *Awakenings* alone to create a culture of engagement in the classroom is to miss opportunities aimed directly at *Strengthening*.

One of the successful *Strengthening* activities Katie does with her students is what she calls "Walks with a Prof." After the first few weeks are over, and after she senses that the previous three steps have worked together to generate significant engagement in the course, Katie invites students in twos or threes to take a walk with her. Each group is assigned to a class period, and on that day they are to meet her at her office 30 minutes before class to walk with her to the building. During these walks, she asks them questions about their lives, especially their relationship to books, ideas, and school. She is interested in hearing about the ways they previously found books inspiring and what they think they can do to be more inspired by books. She also asks them to give feedback on her class. She wants to know how she can make it more engaging and helpful in their pursuit of personal growth and transformation.

Another *Strengthening* activity Katie uses is to invite students who were very successful in the course both academically and socially to return the next semester as "peer-mentors." Peer-mentors attend the course for a second time to facilitate small group discussions and act as tutors for the writing process. Essay writing in Katie's course is rigorous, and she requires students to compose multiple drafts for every paper. Peer-mentors help to build a *Strengthening* culture by affirming the *Hooks*, the *Pitches*, and the *Awakenings* Katie is using in her classroom. Put differently, peer-mentors were the ones who Katie was able to bring to the edge of their seats and who can therefore encourage (implicitly or explicitly) new students to be on the edge of their seats. The peer-mentors are a visual indicator of the power of books—and Katie's class itself—to transform people's lives.

Another *Strengthening* activity Katie uses is to require a consultation with her during office hours (or another time if students can't make office hours). In these consultations, she has students identify strengths, weaknesses, and goals in their reading and writing skills, and also in their "inspiration" skills—that is, the degree to which they approach their readings with transformation in mind. She has students direct the conversations, and she asks them follow-up questions. After the students identify their strengths, weaknesses, and goals for the future, she asks them for their thoughts about how she can improve the course to meet the needs of students.

## *Worksheet for Planning the Four Steps*

Now that we have seen an example of the ways a teacher integrates the four steps over the course of the semester, you can begin thinking about how to plan the four steps on your own. The following worksheet provides some concrete guidance.

| THE HOOK | PLANNING IDEAS |
| --- | --- |
| ***Start with the small things.*** How will I arrange my classroom to communicate the importance of my subject? What will I have on my walls? Where will I be standing or sitting when students arrive at class? How will I arrange the desks? | |
| ***Do something unexpected.*** What can I do in the lead-up and first part of my class that will surprise my students' expectations? Should I go over my syllabus in the second or third class period rather than the first? | |
| ***Put your persona to use.*** How am I going to engage my students to make them curious, confused, consternated, or excited? What aspect of my personality can I bring forth and amplify or diminish to engage them in this way? | |
| ***Foreshadow what's to come.*** How can I allude to and build anticipation toward the content of the course? What is particularly fascinating and exciting about my topic, subject matter, or subject as a whole that I could hint at? | |

| THE PITCH | PLANNING IDEAS |
|---|---|
| ***Express a passion for the subject.*** What am I passionate about in my subject discipline? How can I connect this passion to the topic to be discussed in class? What can I do, or who can I consult, to  increase my passion for the subject? | |
| ***Highlight the intrinsic value of the subject.*** What is particularly fascinating, beautiful, inspiring, or enriching about my subject or the topic? How can I refer to these aspects of the subject matter during the course of my lessons? | |
| ***Play up the mystery.*** What can I say and do to suggest that there is something wondrous, magical, or mysterious about my subject? How can I tell students that they will eventually see this wonder and mystery so as to pique curiosity? | |
| ***Believe in your students.*** Do I really believe that my students are capable of experiencing passion for and deep interest in my subject? If not, what can I do to start believing it? If so, how can I communicate this belief to students? | |

| THE AWAKENING | PLANNING IDEAS |
| --- | --- |
| ***Unsettle students' assumptions.*** What kind of assumptions will the students bring to class? Which ones need to be unsettled before the breakthrough insight can occur? How can I do so in a way that builds tension? | |
| ***Engage their emotions.*** Which emotions "fit" the content of the breakthrough insight best? How can I engage these emotions in students by using dramatic examples, humor, irony, encouragement, suspense, etc.? | |
| ***Create a breakthrough insight.*** Have I carefully planned a culminating moment in the lesson where students recognize the profound significance of the subject matter? Does each step aim at increasing curiosity and positive tension? | |
| ***Make it real.*** What kind of post-insight activities or discussions will deepen and expand the breakthrough moment for students' lives? How much time will students need to "sit" with the insight before applying their thoughts? | |

| THE STRENGTHENING | PLANNING IDEAS |
|---|---|
| **Construct activities that count.** What activities or events can I design and orchestrate to deepen the insights gained in the *Awakening*? Do they connect to students' everyday experience of themselves and the world around them? | |
| **Encourage self-transformation.** How can I encourage my students to develop their sense of agency? How can I support a belief that they can grow as scholars and human beings by means of my subject matter? | |
| **Let students lead.** Have I created assignments where students take the lead? How can I support them in their leadership while also allowing them to lead? | |
| **Invite your students into partnership.** How can I elicit student feedback to improve my course? How can I encourage students to help one another deepen their understanding of the course material? | |

# Conclusion

HAVING DESCRIBED the ways our four-step framework can be used to effectively design a course from the beginning of the term until the end, we want to conclude by discussing some important issues that were briefly addressed in the previous chapters.

## *Using the Four-Step Framework for Planning Individual Lessons*

The first of these is that the four-step framework offered in this book not only applies to the design of quarter-, semester-, or year-long courses, but it also applies to individual lessons that last only a single class period.

Take, for example, Tariq, our physics teacher in Chapter 5. While we used a lesson of his as an example of an *Awakening*, some readers may have noticed that his lesson contained all four steps.

At the beginning of class, Tariq *Hooks* his students by using his persona and expressing calculated incredulity that none of them knew Newton's Second Law of Motion. He mutters *"Unbelievable!"* under his breath. At this moment, Tariq is engaging students by indicating that there is something very important they should know, and yet they do not know it. He then deepens his *Hook* by claiming that not only will they fail the AP exam without this knowledge, but they will also be missing something of incalculable significance for their lives. Here, Tariq is transitioning to the *Pitch*. The *Hook* got their attention, but this added claim suggests that there is something fascinating and intrinsically valuable to be gained in today's lesson. The students, of course, have no idea what the Second Law is or why it is so important, but Tariq is *Pitching* its significance, all the while creating an air of suspense and mystery. (He even claims that physics has something to do with them being able to go to the prom.) Finally, to deepen the *Pitch*, he tells them that he is not going to explain what the Second Law is.

Both the *Hook* and the *Pitch* work together to capture the imaginations of the students and point their attention toward the value of the subject matter. In doing so, they prepare students psychologically for the *Awakening*.

As we saw in his example above, Tariq uses the elevator in the school and some bathroom scales to help the students generate some raw data for analysis. They are to determine how much they weigh when the elevator moves up and how much they weigh when the elevator moves down. This is crucial not only for setting up an *Awakening* concerning the role of "invisible forces" in students' lives, but also for the *Strengthening* exercise that follows. Students are to get into groups, list all the forces impacting them in their lives, and figure out a plan to address them as their "homework." The power of Tariq's lesson lies in its employment of each step of the framework.

This example is not meant to suggest that all steps should be present in every lesson. Teachers will find that various steps of the framework are better emphasized or deemphasized at different times of the year or semester, and given different conditions in the classroom.

For example, we have found that *Hook* and *Pitch* activities often require more time at the beginning of a course, while *Awakening* and *Strengthening* activities come into sharper focus a bit later. This is because teachers generally need to get students to psychologically "buy in" to the course and establish trust with them before they are primed for wholly new perspectives and insights, especially those that may deeply change how they see the world and themselves.

Readers should not take this to be a hard and fast rule, however. We have also found that, even if we successfully *Hook* students in the first several class periods and *Pitch* our subjects to them compellingly, they will often need to be re-*Hooked* or re-*Pitched* later in the course. We can think of a course designed according to the four-step approach as a nested cycle, where each class period will have aspects of the *Hook, Pitch, Awakening* and *Strengthening,* even though the course as a whole may have progressed to a phase in which the teacher wants to focus on a specific step.

## *The Four-Step Framework in Different Cultural Contexts*

Where can teachers apply the four-step framework? Are there contexts in which it won't work, or will be less effective? We have found that the four-step framework works in a wide variety of social and cultural contexts. This does not mean that the four steps will work the same across all cultures, however. One of the most important factors in the success of the four-step framework is understanding what kinds of topics, ideas, framings, stories, or jokes that students will take to heart. Teachers can, of course, never know fully in advance whether their appeals will work. But as long as teachers have the will to find out how their students "tick," their applications of the four-step framework will continually improve. Their acquaintance with students' personalities will grow over time so that the process will get easier the more the teacher understands the students.

As an example, one of us (Doug) teaches and works at a university in Germany. German university students have very different expectations than Americans about what their professors are supposed to do in the classroom. The relationship between teacher and student tends to be very distant and impersonal; the pedagogy is usually no-frills. Expectations like these should not—and in Doug's case do not—*dictate* what we do in the classroom, of course, but it is essential to know just how far outside of student expectations we are at any given time. We have found that it helps students occasionally to say things like, "Now, I know this is going to sound crazy, but ….." or "You've never had a professor do X, but that's just what I'm going to do" or "Now, this will feel a little awkward, but I promise it will pay off."

These statements may seem subtle or insignificant, but they are essential for reassuring students that we understand what is being asked of them—that we may be making them feel uncertain, surprised, or uncomfortable. And this helps students open their minds to novel kinds of experiences and activities in the classroom. When we are operating outside students' comfort zones, it is vital to offer this kind of re-assurance from time to time, and especially to get regular feedback regarding whether our attempts are working.

In fact, we should mention again that the four-step frame-work will almost certainly fail to be effective if teachers do not find ways to elicit frequent feedback from students. Teachers will never have enough knowledge of students for their appeals to land correctly every time, and this is especial-ly the case when there are racial, cultural, ethnic, religious, and philosophical differences between teachers and students. We think these differences can be—must be—bridged in the classroom. But to make sure we are doing this correctly, we have to hear students' own voices on the matter. We do not necessarily mean the end-of-course "feedback survey" like the ones common in college, though these are certainly part of the story. Rather, we mean things like Terrell's advisory boards. It could be as simple as going for a regular walk with a few students at a time, eating lunch with the class in the cafeteria, setting up regular one-on-one "pedagogy talks," or asking students to give *you* a grade at the end of every unit.

There are countless ways to get valuable feedback from students. The only requirement is that the method one chooses pairs well with one's persona.

## *Learning to Love Your Subject Matter and Your Students*

In our discussion until now, two important characteristics about exceptional teachers have remained implicit. The most effective educators love the discipline they teach, and they love their students. These two kinds of love are essential for each and every step of the framework. If students sense that one of them is missing, then the four steps will simply not work.

Take James, our English teacher who served as an example of the *Hook*. James' *Hook* clearly communicates his love for his subject matter and his passion for English, which is a necessary component of the *Pitch*. His classroom arrangement, even down to the way he situated desks, was supposed to exhibit the value of discussion and ideas in the classroom. Moreover, even though his opening question wasn't directly about literature, the way he prowled around the room and expected deep and thoughtful answers about freedom strongly suggested that he believed something really important was going on in class. If James did not love his subject matter, he would not have been as committed to his approach; he would have been merely acting, and his students would have sensed it.

Similarly, James's love for his students was equally present. Again, the way he arranged his desks to facilitate conversation and the way he expected them to think deeply about freedom demonstrated his belief in them as reasoners and people. Students left his class a little shell-shocked by the unusual approach he took in class, but they also left with at least the subconscious awareness that James believed what was going to be happening in his classroom was of the utmost importance. James was certain that his students were entirely capable of recognizing this same importance and participating in bringing that importance to life. We saw the same emphasis in Mariela's science class. She made it clear that she loved science and that she believed in her students' ability to experience and participate in that love for themselves. In believing in her students in this way, she, like James, was showing love to her students.

What do teachers do if they just don't love their subject matter or their students in the way James or Mariela do? Is there any way these teachers can bring students to the edge of their seats?

In one sense, the answer to this question is no. Students who are on the edge of their seats are students whose imaginations have been captured by the teacher and the subject matter. They want to be in class, and they know that something significant might happen at any moment. For students to feel this way about class, they have to know that their teacher feels the same way.

However, we believe that the framework outlined in this book offers hope to the teacher who does not love their subject or their students. Obviously, the book is premised on the fact that the subjects we teach in schools are intrinsically lovable. We believe that students *can* become fascinated by academic subject matter, and they *will* become fascinated if teachers use *Hooks, Pitches, Awakenings,* and *Strengthenings* in the way we have suggested. Because academic subject matter is itself intrinsically fascinating, then, in theory, any teacher can grow to love it. Like the example of Jenn, the math teacher in Chapter 4, teachers can develop a love for their subject matter as they seek to discover what is lovable about it. And its lovability becomes increasingly apparent as they begin to express it to their students.

The same can be said about loving students. Even though they are sometimes disengaged, distracted, or disruptive, students are—by virtue of being individual human beings—intrinsically fascinating. It is a mystery why students think the way they think and do the things they do. Students are like a riddle that can be partially "solved" if teachers employ the four-step framework. However, solving the riddle of student engagement does not mean that they become less fascinating. Once they are deeply engaged in our courses, students exhibit new sides of themselves. They become partners in learning and self-transformation along with us. When we succeed in this way, it is one of the most satisfying, enjoyable, and life-giving aspects of being a teacher.

## *The Point of This Book*

We have just claimed that teaching can be deeply satisfying and fulfilling. We have discovered this to be true in our own classrooms and have met countless teachers who have found it to be true in theirs. While, on the one hand, we hope this book has provided teachers with a way of structuring their courses and planning their lessons that will bring students to the edge of their seats, we also wish to remind teachers of just how life-giving teaching can be. At its worst, teaching can be one of the most difficult, frustrating, and draining careers a person can have. But at its best, teaching can be joyful, fascinating, and profoundly fulfilling. We hope that the four-step framework offered in this book will inspire some and re-inspire others to discover the joys of teaching.

# 9

# Frequently Asked Questions

*Do the Four Steps Increase
Teacher Professionalism?*

ONE OF THE FIRST concepts teachers encounter in their licensure programs is teacher professionalism. Typically, "professionalism" serves as a kind of umpire concept. It tells teachers when their conduct with students, administrators, parents, and guardians is ethically safe or out of bounds, and it urges them to conform to the social and institutional expectations that govern teachers' behavior. It hardly needs to be said that this sense of professionalism is very important. We rightly want to know when our actions may be out of line. But there is also a danger in allowing this understanding to dominate what teacher professionalism means. We can lose sight of a more expansive notion of professionalism that is less about following rules and more about achieving professional excellence. This idea of professionalism involves embodying certain attitudes, beliefs, and practices that elevate our teaching, make us better colleagues, encourage us to treat parents more respectfully, and inspire us to help students become the best people they can be. To be a professional means not merely following a list of rules that are dictated by the school or district, but about committing to students so sincerely that our actions and decisions at every professional level seek to increase students' well-being and flourishing. It is about *loving* what we do.[19]

This fuller notion of professionalism captures more of the essence of professional practice than does the traditional umpire conception. Professions like teaching, law, and medicine are different from other vocations in their embodiment of an *ethic of service*.[20] To embody an ethic of service, professionals must have certain *feelings* toward those served and toward one's own professional practice. Everyone has had a doctor whose heart just isn't in it, and it is generally an unpleasant experience. The best doctors are the ones who truly care about their patients, who are fascinated by medicine, and who love what they do. The same is true of teachers. If teachers don't care about students' growth as people, or if they don't feel fulfilled in providing this care, they may be offering *instruction*, but they will never truly *teach*. In other words, they have not fully risen to a professional level of practice. This is the case even if the teacher is successful in helping students meet their learning targets. Meeting learning targets without helping students to become their best selves or develop a meaningful relationship to the subject matter is not professional teaching as it was meant to be.

How can teachers exhibit this kind of professionalism toward their students? The only answer that seems compelling to us is by showing students how their subject matter can enrich and expand their personal horizons in the most comprehensive way possible. If we ignore how our subjects can speak to our students' unique personalities, if we ignore our students' aspirations and ideals, or if we only want to increase their academic knowledge, then we have made an important mistake. We have not yet become professionals in the fullest and most rewarding sense of that term. The four-step framework provides a model for achieving professionalism in teaching in a comprehensive way.

## *Do the Four Steps Increase Intrinsic Motivation?*

The topic of motivation is well-known among teachers. In teacher education courses, nearly all teachers learn (or relearn) the difference between *intrinsic* and *extrinsic* motivation. The standard view is that while *extrinsic* motivation often helps motivate students to complete learning tasks, the holy grail of motivation is *intrinsic* in nature. Intrinsically motivated students want to learn things for their own sake. They pursue learning not to earn a gold star, gain their teacher's approval, or receive an "A," but simply because they have an interest in the subject matter.

This common view is not quite right. According to the research, *intrinsic* motivation arises only when students pursue activities completely of their own accord.[21] In education, this is almost never possible. Rather, teachers should strive for *internal* motivation, which occurs when teachers offer something to students' interest, and they respond by recognizing its personal significance and objective importance. For example, students who become fascinated with a subject at school because of the teacher's use of the four-step framework, they are not intrinsically motivated, because they did not arrive at school on the first day already fascinated. However, the student *experiences* this new motivation as intrinsic, since they have internalized the value of the subject matter. But technically speaking, the motivation is internal, not intrinsic. The important point is that whatever we call it—intrinsic or internal—students who experience this kind of motivation perform better on content-related assessments; they are far less likely to cheat; they enjoy their experience in school more; and they are more resilient in the face of challenges.

So how can we create internal motivation in our classrooms? To answer this question, we first need to understand *what* we are activating inside the student when they become internally motivated. One simple way of thinking about this is to see students as possessing three related but distinct powers. Students have the power of *feeling, thinking,* and *knowing*. Students' *feelings* are constantly coloring the way they experience the world and what happens in the classroom. Their *thinking* draws their attention this way or that, whether toward the subject matter and related tasks or toward other things. And their *knowing*—or, knowledge-related beliefs—provide a cognitive foundation so that their experiences in the classroom lead to learning. When students are internally motivated, their feelings, thoughts, and knowledge-related beliefs are all directed toward the teacher's instructional activities. They are emotionally invested in the subject matter, their minds are determined to understand it, and they are engaged in using their prior learning to complete the tasks at hand. If students' feelings and thoughts wander to other things in the classroom, or if we fail to convince students that the subject matter is exciting and worth thinking about, then the learning that occurs will be fleeting and superficial.

Recognizing these three basic powers leads to an important insight: If we want students to be fully engaged in our classes, we have to structure our classes and plan our lessons with their feelings, thoughts, and knowledge-related beliefs in the front of our minds. Put simply, teachers need to be *psychologists* who are constantly trying to figure out how pedagogical choices will holistically impact their students. We have to ask ourselves: what are our students *feeling* right now, and how can I harness these emotions for their learning? What are they *thinking* about, and how can we get their thoughts focused on the subject matter? What do they *know* or *believe*, and how can we challenge or confirm this prior knowledge and capture their imagination? In essence, the four-step framework is designed to help teachers answer these questions and address students' three basic powers in a systematic way. When teachers do so, they create a powerful form of internal motivation in students that often persists even beyond the classroom walls.

## *Do the Four Steps Support Lifelong Learning?*

It might seem a truism to say that the essence of teaching revolves around how much students learn or fail to learn in the classroom. Indeed, these days, it is quite common for students to be referred to as "learners" rather than students or pupils. On the one hand, this makes sense. We *do* want students to learn in school—to be so impacted by their educational experiences that they become lifelong learners. The problem is that accomplishing this goal requires several different levels and kinds of learning, and these tend to get crowded out by the pressure to meet academic learning objectives and increase test performance.

To help students become lifelong learners, we believe schools should be sites of the richest learning possible, which includes everything from gaining important life skills, meeting academic learning objectives, performing well on grade-level assessments, achieving self-efficacy as learners, and developing key academic skills. However, learning holistically understood means also growing in a sense of wonder, gaining a deeper appreciation of beauty, recognizing the value of others, and becoming better citizens at the global and local level, to name just a few. If we only succeed in helping students meet a level of competence in academic subject matter, we have done them, ourselves, and our community a disservice. The school may be able to publicize high levels of student proficiency on their websites, and in that sense, the school will look like an exemplary place of learning—but the students will not be getting what they deserve.

Part of the reason students don't learn all that they are capable of learning is simply because we teachers forget that young people have so much potential. Teachers talk a lot about having "high standards," believing in their students' "potential," and having an "asset perspective," but often these phrases revolve around students' ability to "hit learning targets," "grow as readers" or "develop social and emotional competencies." These efforts are very important, of course, and the best teachers can make students believe that they can accomplish these goals regardless of their background or current skill level. However, the best teachers do more than just that. When students leave their classes, they not only think that they are capable of "doing well in school," or "getting better at math," or "achieving an A." They also believe they can make a difference in the world and become better people than they were when they started the school year.

The teachers who have the greatest impact on students don't just focus on academic learning targets; they also genuinely believe that their students are capable of loving the subject matter and of using the comprehensive knowledge and skills that they gain to make a difference in the world. When students sense that their teachers expect and believe that they can, for example, love math or science or history for its own sake, students are far more likely to believe it themselves, and begin to try to do so. Students can and want to believe that they are not just people who display certain competencies or have good study habits, but whose full power and potential is awakened by their educational experiences. When this happens, students become lifelong learners. This is why steps three and four of the framework—the *Awakening* and the *Strengthening*—are so crucial for successful classrooms. They make sure that students see the connections between subject matter and their own personal striving to live a full life.

## Do the Four Steps Advance Educational Equity?

Bringing students to the edge of their seats is not just a

pedagogical task; it is a political one too. When teachers engage students at the highest level, a special kind of community forms in their classrooms. They give students something they can share in spite of their differences—namely, a love of learning. This love of learning is one of the most powerful means that teachers have available to them to unite diverse students. In our view, this sense of unity is just what we need at this political moment.

This unity is also essential for advancing educational equity. We know from decades of sociological research that disadvantaged students and students of color have less access to stimulating and challenging academic environments. Their potential is more often misunderstood or undersold by our educational system.[22] Teachers who awaken a common love of learning in their classrooms counteract these trends. They contribute, if only in a small way, to creating a more just society.

This does not mean that the four steps outlined in this book are a cure-all. There are many systemic issues in the American education system that cannot immediately be addressed by the work of individual teachers. There are parts of the education system that need to be reevaluated and changed in order to meet the needs of *all* students, no matter their educational or cultural experiences. This book does not address these detrimental systemic issues in the comprehensive manner they require. However, it offers teachers strategies to make their classrooms places of extraordinary learning for all students. We believe these strategies can serve as a foundation for the broader structural changes that need to be made in our educational system.

## *Are the Four Steps Helpful for Increasing Academic Performance?*

One of the most important factors for increasing academic performance is teachers' relationships to the subjects they teach. When teachers decide to become teachers at the secondary or post-secondary level, they are always choosing to become a teacher *of something*. Teachers study physics or chemistry or English literature so that they can teach young people what these subjects have to offer. Unfortunately, something often happens during teacher education that can seriously undermine teachers' effectiveness. While they might have begun with a real passion for their discipline, teachers can start to think of their disciplines merely as repositories of skills and knowledge necessary for students to graduate from high school or college. In other words, they forget just how fascinating and life-giving their subjects can be.

This kind of development is a serious problem for ensuring high levels of academic performance. Academic subjects are more than repositories of useful skills and knowledge. They have compelling disciplinary histories, full of exciting personalities and thrilling tales of discovery and deception. They have special vocabularies and unique ways of communicating ideas. They celebrate profound formulas and findings, and honor the hard-won accomplishments of thinkers, scientists, activists, and writers. They are also home to a contemporary community of inquirers who share a fascination for the subject matter. Often, these aspects alone—if they are properly illuminated in the classroom—are enough to get students engaged much more deeply than they would be otherwise.

Our subjects are not only products of exciting histories or committed communities of like-minded individuals, however. They also help us unlock the beauty, mystery, and wonder of the world around us. For example, students typically think about math as something we "do," and a math class as a place we go to solve math problems. But there are people who have come to a different understanding of math altogether. These are individuals whose teachers made math come alive for them, teachers who showed them how elegant a proof or profound a theorem could be. The same goes for science. There are teachers who make science so interesting that students start looking at things differently and appreciate the natural world in a way they never had before. This kind of transformation can happen in any subject area. Literature teachers can transform a formerly "boring" book into one that students love so much that they talk about it with their friends and family. History teachers can turn historical figures into living, breathing people with whom students genuinely empathize and engage.

When teachers bring out the beauty, mystery, and wonder of their subject matter in this way, students not only are far more likely to achieve academic learning targets, but they are also less likely to engage in disruptive behaviors while in class.[23] These facts alone would make the kind of teaching we are describing desirable. But from the students' point of view, the most important reason for teachers to bring out the intrinsic value of their subject matter is that students feel more alive in these classes, and they often carry that feeling with them outside of class. When this happens, the subjects we teach enrich students' experience in ways that can have a positive impact on the rest of their lives.

When we talk about enhancing academic performance nowadays, we so often miss this richer sense of what true "performance" really entails. It is not merely success at reproducing academic knowledge, but also the ability to see and feel the wonder of the subject matter. Enhancing academic performance means expanding students' emotional and experiential horizons by engaging with the vibrant life of the discipline.

## Are the Four Steps Suitable for Diverse Classrooms?

One of the most important and challenging aspects of teaching in the 21st century is the wide diversity of students in our classrooms. More than ever, our classes are heterogeneous. Teaching students from different ethnicities, religions, sexual or gender orientations, cultural backgrounds, and intellectual capacities—to name just a few categories—makes the job exciting, but also extremely challenging. One-size-fits-all approaches to teaching simply do not work today, if indeed they ever worked.

It is tempting, therefore, to come up with a "multiple-sizes-fit-all" approach to teaching in diverse classrooms. In this approach, teachers make assumptions about the students they teach based on gender, ethnicity, race, religion, sexuality, and so on. They rely on stereotypes gathered from sociology textbooks, movies, and other sources to develop strategies that work for "these types of students." This might seem to be a form of "student-centered" pedagogy, but it is in fact potentially quite damaging to students' own identities. Students can feel pigeonholed into a caricature of who they are based on assumptions about their racial or cultural background. They can feel reduced to one aspect of their identity rather than being appreciated for their full personality or character.

How can teachers reach each of their students in a way that honors their individuality? Part of the advantage of the four-step framework we offer in this book is that it is meant to be flexible enough for use with any demographic makeup, any subject matter, and within any subject discipline. By bringing in the aspects of the subject beyond just "knowledge"—the rich history of a discipline, the personalities involved, the rituals practiced, and the ideas celebrated—and by helping students see how these seemingly foreign ways of perceiving the world can actually enrich their own unique perspectives, teachers can help students connect with the subject matter in ways never before imagined. This, in turn, allows students to find their own diverse interests and skills reflected in the subject matter.

# Endnotes



**1** Appleton et al. (2008) indicate the near universality of this experience. "The importance of student engagement with school is recognized by educators, as is the observation that far too many students are bored, unmotivated, and un-involved, that is, disengaged from the academic and social aspects of school life" (p. 369). James J. Appleton, Sandra L. Christenson, Michael J. Furlong, "Student Engagement with School: Critical Conceptual and Methodological Issues of the Construct," *Psychology in the Schools* 45, no. 5 (2008): 369–86.

**2** There is extensive research on the problem of student disengagement and the strategies teachers and schools can use to help engage students in their learning. Much of this research has been collected into several comprehensive handbooks. See Amy L. Reschly, Angie J. Pohl, and Sandra L. Christenson, *Student Engagement: Effective Academic, Behavioral, Cognitive, and Affective Interventions at School* (Cham,

Switzerland: Springer, 2020); Sandra L. Christenson, Amy L. Reschly, and Cathy Wylie, Handbook of Research on Student Engagement (New York: Springer, 2012); Committee on Increasing High School Students' Engagement and Motivation to Learn, *Engaging Schools: Fostering High School Students' Motivation to Learn* (Washington, DC: National Academic Press, 2004).

**3** When we use the term disengagement or disengaged, we mean a psychological state in which students are not interested in what they are learning and display little motivation to become interested. In this we follow Fredricks, Blumenfeld, and Paris (2004), who identified three forms of engagement: behavioral engagement, emotional engagement, and cognitive engagement. We believe that all three modes of engagement must be present for students to be genuinely engaged. Thus, a student who diligently completes all their assignments but does so with no interest or inspiration may look engaged, but they are disengaged in their emotional experience. The four steps we outline in this book support teachers in creating all three types of engagement. Jennifer A. Fredricks, Phyllis C. Blumenfeld, & Alison H. Paris, "School Engagement: Potential of the Concept, State of the Evidence," *Review of Educational Research* 74, no. 1 (2004): 59–109.

**4** Committee on Increasing High School Students' Engagement and Motivation to Learn, *Engaging Schools*, 211.

**5** Jung-Sook Lee, "The Relationship between Student Engagement and Academic Performance: Is It a Myth or Reality?" *The Journal of Educational Research* 107, no. 3 (2014): 177–185. Dale H. Schunk, "Self-Efficacy and Achievement Behaviors," Educational Psychology Review 1 (1989): 173–208. Dale H. Schunk & Carol A. Mullen, "Self-Efficacy as an Engaged Learner," *Handbook of Research on Student Engagement* (Cham, Switzerland: Springer, 2012): 219–235. Tim Hodges, "School Engagement Is More Than Just Talk," Gallup, October 25, 2018, https://www.gallup.com/education/244022/school-engagement-talk.aspx.

**6** "In addition to having greater burdens and distractions, the consequences of being unengaged or dropping out of school are more serious for youth who do not have the social and other resources available to cushion the effects of academic failure." Committee on Increasing High School Students' Engagement and Motivation to Learn, *Engaging Schools*, 211.

**7** Committee on Increasing High School Students' Engagement and Motivation to Learn, *Engaging Schools*, 60.

**8** See, for example: Kevin J. Pugh, *Transformative Science Education: Change How Your Students Experience the World* (New York: Teachers College Press, 2020); Andrea R. English, *Discontinuity in Learning: Dewey, Herbart, and Education as Transformation* (New York: Cambridge University Press, 2014); Jack Mezirow, *Learning as Transformation: Critical Perspectives on a Theory in Progress* (San Francisco: Jossey-Bass, 2000).

**9** Kevin J. Pugh, "Teaching for Idea-Based, Transformative Experiences in Science: An Investigation of the Effectiveness of Two Instructional Elements," *Teachers College Record* 104, no. 6 (2002): 1101–37. Douglas W. Yacek, *The Transformative Classroom: Philosophical Foundations and Practical Applications* (London: Routledge, 2019). David Sill, Brian M. Harward and Ivy Cooper, "The Disorienting Dilemma: The Senior Capstone as a Transformative Experience," *Liberal Education* 95, no. 3 (2009): 50–55.

**10** Kevin J. Pugh, "Transformative Experience: An Integrative Construct in the Spirit of Deweyan Pragmatism," *Educational Psychologist* 46, no. 2 (2011): 107–21.

**11** Pugh, *Transformative Science Education*. Yacek, *The Transformative Classroom*.

**12** Kevin J. Pugh, Lisa Linnenbrink-Garcia, Kristin L. K. Koskey, Victoria C. Stewart, and Christine Manzey, "Motivation, Learning, and Transformative Experience: A Study of Deep Engagement in Science," *Science Education* 94, no. 1 (2010a): 1–28. Kevin J. Pugh, Lisa Linnenbrink-Garcia, Kristin L. K. Koskey, Victoria C. Stewart & Christine Manzey, "Teaching for Transformative Experiences and Conceptual Change: A Case Study and Evaluation of a High School Biology Teacher's Experience," *Cognition and Instruction* 28, no. 3 (2010b): 273–316.

**13** The research on transformative teaching has shown that two instructional methods have proven to be especially effective for creating these kinds of experiences: modeling and scaffolding. In modeling, the teacher embodies the transformation of perspective that he or she hopes to bring about. This is reflected especially in the second step of our framework: the Pitch. In scaffolding, the teacher carefully leads students toward this perspective incrementally, often with the help of surprising and unexpected actions or activities. This is reflected in the third step of our framework: the *Awakening.* Pugh, *Transformative Science Education.*

## 2. GETTING STARTED WITH THE FRAMEWORK

**14** The desire to be challenged is an essential component for students to be authentically motivated. Richard M. Ryan and Edward L. Deci, "Self-Determination Theory and the Facilitation of Intrinsic Motivation, Social Development, and Well-Being," *American Psychologist* 55, no. 2 (2000): 71.

**15** Ryan and Deci have found that there is a significant difference between "people whose motivation is authentic (literally, self-authored or endorsed) and those who are merely externally controlled." Those whose motivation is authentic have "more interest, excitement, and confidence, which in turn is manifest both as enhanced performance, persistence, and creativity;...and as heightened vitality,...self-esteem, and general well-being." Ryan and Deci, "Self-Determination Theory," 69. Motivation can be authentic in at least two ways. Ryan and Deci write that it can be "self-authored," which means it literally arises spontaneously in the self, or it can be "endorsed," which means it arises from an external source, like a teacher, but becomes "integrated" as one's own. They claim that "integration occurs when identified regulations are fully assimilated into the self, which means they have been evaluated and brought into congruence with one's other values and needs." Ryan and Deci, "Self-Determination Theory," 73.

**16** In responding to this culture, students "seek out novelty and challenges, to extend and exercise one's capacities, to explore, and to learn." Ryan and Deci, "Self-Determination Theory," 70.

**17** Students' need for agency and autonomy has been well supported by Ryan and Deci's extremely influential Self-Determination Theory. According to their theory, students learn more effectively when they are internally motivated to learn the material rather than being motivated externally. Setting a high academic bar for students and helping them to believe they can reach that bar increases internal motivation and self-determination. Richard M. Ryan and Edward L. Deci, *Self-Determination Theory: Basic Psychological Needs in Motivation, Development, and Wellness.* (New York: Guilford Press, 2017).

## 4. THE PITCH

**18** Kenneth A. Strike, "Trust, Traditions and Pluralism: Human Flourishing and Liberal Polity," *Virtue Ethics and Moral Education* (London, England: Routledge, 2005): 231–244.

## 9. FREQUENTLY ASKED QUESTIONS

**19** For an extended critique of the umpire notion of professionalism, see: Chris Higgins, *The Good Life of Teaching: An Ethics of Professional Practice* (Malden, MA: John Wiley & Sons, 2011).

**20** For an excellent discussion of this aspect of professionalism, see Bruce A. Kimball, *The „True Professional Ideal" in America: A History* (Lanham, MD: Rowman & Littlefield, 1996).

**21** Ryan and Deci, "Self-Determination Theory," 69-73.

**22** See, for example, Richard Rothstein, *Class and Schools: Using Social, Economic, and Educational Reform to Close the Black-White Achievement Gap* (New York: Teachers College, 2004); Sean Nicholson-Crotty, Jason A. Grissom, Jill Nicholson-Crotty, and Cristopher Redding, "Disentangling the Causal Mechanisms of Representative Bureaucracy: Evidence from Assignment of Students to Gifted Programs," *Journal of Public Administration Research and Theory* 26, no. 4 (2016): 745–757; Paul L. Morgan, George Farkas, Michael Cook, Natasha M. Strassfeld, Marianne M. Hillemeier, Wik Hung Pun and Deborah L. Schussler, "Are Black Children Disproportionately Overrepresented in Special Education? A Best-Evidence Synthesis," *Exceptional Children* 83, no. 2 (2017): 181–198.

**23** See Jung-Sook Lee, "The Relationship between Student Engagemnt and Academic Performance: Is It a Myth or Reality?" *The Journal of Educational Research* 107, no. 3 (2014): 177–185. Also see Terrance M. Scott, Regina G. Hirn, and Peter J. Alter, "Teacher Instruction as a Predictor for Student Engagement and Disruptive Behaviors," *Preventing School Failure: Alternative Education for Children and Youth* 58, no. 4 (2014): 193–200.